Short Plays with Great R
for Women

Short Plays with Great Roles for Women is an antidote to the traditional under-representation of women on stage, by offering twenty-two short plays that put women right at the centre of the action.

The push for more women's roles has gathered force over the last few years, and this collection is part of that movement, with rich, intelligent roles for women of all ages and backgrounds. This anthology offers a vital slice of life, addressing relevant and diverse topics such as: a young, Islamic woman coming out to her religious mother; black women's navigation of the natural hair movement; bullying in a small-town American school; social media addiction; and the trials and tribulations of family life. Plays from award-winning playwrights are supported by original production details and playwrights' afterwords, forming a broad and comprehensive collection of complete texts that offer full character journeys.

Appealing to aspiring performers, playwrights, directors and students, *Short Plays with Great Roles for Women* is an essential resource for actor training, assessments, showcases, show-reels, short films and theatre performances.

Suzette Coon is a playwright and artistic director of Little Pieces of Gold theatre company. Her plays have been produced at theatres across London, and since 2010 she has produced the short plays of over 400 emerging, established and award-winning playwrights.

Short Plays with Great Roles for Women

Edited by Suzette Coon

 Routledge
Taylor & Francis Group

LONDON AND NEW YORK

First published 2020
by Routledge
2 Park Square, Milton Park, Abingdon, Oxon OX14 4RN

and by Routledge
52 Vanderbilt Avenue, New York, NY 10017

Routledge is an imprint of the Taylor & Francis Group, an informa business

British Library Cataloguing-in-Publication Data
A catalogue record for this book is available from the British Library

Library of Congress Cataloging-in-Publication Data
A catalog record has been requested for this book

ISBN: 978-0-367-18711-8 (hbk)
ISBN: 978-0-367-18713-2 (pbk)
ISBN: 978-0-429-19780-2 (ebk)

Typeset in Times New Roman
by Wearset Ltd, Boldon, Tyne and Wear

MIX
Paper from
responsible sources
FSC
www.fsc.org   FSC™ C013985

Printed in the United Kingdom
by Henry Ling Limited

To the ones who make the unknown known

Contents

Contributors

Stella Ajayi is a playwright and screenwriter based in London. Stella was a part of the 2018/2019 Hampstead Theatre Inspire Playwright Program under the mentorship of playwright Roy Williams. She has had work produced at Southwark Playhouse, Theatre Peckham, Lion and Unicorn Theatre, Bunker Theatre, and Bernie Grant Arts Centre. Stella has performed stand-up comedy open mic nights in London since 2016. She is also a script reader for The Upsetters, a series of short play nights for writers and creatives of colour in London. She has worked at The Old Vic and Tamasha Theatre Company.

Laura Jayne Ayres is an actor and playwright from Leeds. She graduated from Cambridge University and joined the rural touring company NTC Touring Theatre as an actor, and later worked with them as a writer. *Consolea* is Laura's first short play and she is currently developing it into a full-length script. Her second short play *Escape*, based on the song 'Escape' (The Piña Colada Song), was also shown at Southwark Playhouse as part of Little Pieces of Gold in 2018. 'Olso', an extract from the full *Consolea* play, was shown at The Pleasance in 2018 as part of A Night of Small Things, and another short play, *Mabel*, was performed at the Lion and Unicorn Theatre in 2019 as part of Round Peg Theatre's HATCH.

Dipo Baruwa-Etti is a playwright and poet. His work has been showcased at theatres, including The Yard Theatre, Arcola Theatre, Old Vic Workrooms and Southwark Playhouse. In 2018, he was shortlisted for BBC Drama Room and 4Stories, and longlisted for the Royal Court Theatre/Kudos Fellowship. As a poet, Dipo has been published in *The Good Journal*, *Amaryllis*, and had his work tour nationwide as part of End Hunger UK's exhibition on food insecurity.

Fran Bushe is an award-winning performer, playwright and comedian. Her work has been performed at Soho Theatre, The Roundhouse, and she has been resident artist at The Pleasance, Arts Depot and Theatre Deli. Fran's solo show *Ad Libido* had a sold-out run in Edinburgh 2019 and a run at Soho Theatre in May 2019. Her first play *The Site* won a Hampstead Theatre playwriting competition and was performed at The Roundhouse. She writes and regularly performs with an all-female sketch group Kitten Killers who have had award-nominated sold-out runs at Soho Theatre and Underbelly, Edinburgh. She is an experienced lyricist and went on to write the book and lyrics for the musical *Sunny Spells*. Her short plays are regularly performed at Theatre503, Southwark Playhouse, Oval House and New Diorama Theatre.

Grace Ivana Carroll is a London playwright and graduated with a Screenwriting MA from London College of Communication. She often writes stories with female protagonists that tackle serious topics in a light-hearted manner. Grace's short plays have been performed at theatres across London, including Theatre503, Bunker Theatre, Tristan Bates Theatre, Southwark Playhouse and Theatre N16. Her short play, *Swipe*, was selected for Little Pieces of Gold in January 2018. Her full-length play *Wet*, a comedy about two friends who try to make a feminist porn film, received productions at London's Theatre N16 and Amsterdam's Perdu Theatre.

Vicki Connerty spent several glorious years working in the Australian media industry before returning from Sydney to her native London in 2016 to study at the Royal Central School of Speech and Drama, graduating in 2017 with an MA (Distinction) in Writing for the Stage and Broadcast Media. *Come Die With Me* is Vicki's debut short play, a tragi-comedy inspired by the death of her beloved father some fifteen years earlier. It has received numerous productions on the UK new writing circuit and was selected for international festivals in Los Angeles, Sydney and Dubai. *Come Die With Me* has evolved into a full-length play called *The Vigil* under the mentorship of British playwright Amy Rosenthal, and Vicki has recently completed her second full-length play, *The Snow Angel of Antarctica*. She is currently working on her first script for television.

Gabrielle Curtis is a writer and actress. She trained at Drama Centre London during which time she studied the Writing and Directing pathways. She also worked independently as a writer as part of the school's Movement Psychology programme. Gabrielle's professional writing credits include: Bonus of Contention; *The Artistically Protected Right to Over-React*; *A Meaningful, Albeit Brief, Encounter* (Old Red Lion); *After* as part of The Millennials at Southwark Playhouse (for which she was mentored by playwright and screenwriter Vinay Patel) and *SLAM* at The Pleasance. For screen, Gabrielle wrote and produced a short film, *Closure*. *The Petal and The Orchid* marks herself and Clare Joy Langford's first enterprise as a writing partnership, and was first shown at Southwark Playhouse (for Little Pieces of Gold) and then again at The Old Red Lion Theatre and Southwark Playhouse (for Underexposed:2).

Fiona Doyle's work in theatre includes *Coolatully* (winner of the 2014 Papatango New Writing Prize) at the Finborough Theatre in London and for Mead Theatre Lab in Washington, DC; *Deluge* (winner of the 2014 Eamon Keane Full-Length Play Award) and *The Strange Death of John Doe* (2018 Susan

Smith Blackburn Prize Finalist) at Hampstead Theatre Downstairs; *The Anni-hilation of Jessie Leadbeater* (ALRA); *The Ceasefire Babies* (NT Connec-tions) and *Ms Y* (short) as part of the Young Vic's Five Plays. Fiona has been the recipient of the Irish Theatre Institute's Phelim Donlon Playwright's Bursary and Residency Award in association with the Tyrone Guthrie Centre, a Cill Rialaig Artist residency, a Peggy Ramsay Foundation grant, a Mac-Dowell Colony Fellowship (subsequently being selected for honorary desig-nation as a Stanford Calderwood Fellow for 2018), and an attachment at the National Theatre Studio. She is currently under commission to the Bridge Theatre and is developing an original idea for TV with Adorable Media. Her work is published by Nick Hern Books and Methuen Drama.

Sarah Hehir was born in Scunthorpe, England, and studied Drama at Manches-ter University. She writes drama and poetry for TV, radio and the stage. She was recently presented with an Arts Council England award to work with artists in both the UK and Kosovo to develop collaborative theatre in evolv-ing spaces. In 2013, she won the inaugural BBC Writer's Prize for her drama *Bang Up*, and in 2016, her TV drama *The Seafort* was selected for the BBC TV Drama Writers' Programme. Her stage plays *Child Z*, *Zero Down*, *Echoes Through the Dust*, *March* and *Son of a Precariat* have been performed in London at Theatre503, Southwark Playhouse and The Park Theatre. In 2016, *Zero Down* was transferred to The Pleasance, Edinburgh Fringe Festival. She leads creative writing workshops in prisons, theatres, schools and universities. Her poems have been published in *Confluence* and *Bare Fiction Magazine* and she performs them at national and international literary festivals. She is currently developing a new stage play and writing for BBC Doctors.

Tatty Hennessy is an award-winning playwright, dramaturg and director. In 2017 she won the Heretic Voices Monologue Competition with her play *A Hundred Words for Snow* which was produced by Heretic Voices at the Arcola Theatre in January 2018. The play transferred to the Trafalgar Studios in March 2019 following a short UK tour, where it received four Offie nomi-nations, including Best New Play and Most Promising New Playwright. In 2018, Tatty was commissioned to write *F* OFF* for the National Youth Theatre. Previously she has adapted *The Snow Queen* for Theatre N16, developed her first play *All That Lives* about Henrietta Lacks at the Oval-house Theatre and took part in The Park Theatre Script Accelerator Pro-gramme with her play *Scum*.

Yasmin Joseph was one of Theatre503's resident playwrights, The 503Five. Here she developed her debut play *J'Ouvert* which received a production in May 2019. Yasmin is also an alumna of Soho Theatre Young Writers Lab. Other theatre credits include *Rumble* (Gate Theatre: Harrow Club Company), *Sugar* (Kiln Theatre: Mapping Brent), as well as short plays, *The Place of Shining Light* (Theatre503) and *Do You Pray?* (Theatre503 and Southwark Playhouse).

Sarah Kosar is an internationally produced and published playwright. Originally from Butler, Pennsylvania, she moved to London to pursue playwriting following her graduation from Penn State University with a BA in Theatre and a BA in Film. In 2011, she received her MA in Writing for Stage and Broadcast Media from the Royal Central School of Speech and Drama in London. In 2015, she was granted an Exceptional Promise in Playwriting visa. She was named the Inaugural Writer in Residence at The Archivist's Gallery in 2016 and selected as one of the Old Vic 12 for 2017/2018. Sarah's full-length plays include *Armadillo* (The Yard Theatre), *Our Name is Not John* (Reading as part of Old Vic 12, Old Vic Theatre), *Mumburger* (Old Red Lion, The Archivist's Gallery, off the WALL productions – American Premiere), *Hot Dog* (The Last Refuge – London, Thinking Cap Theatre – Florida, USA), *Spaghetti Ocean* (Reading as part of Live Lunch season, Royal Court Theatre), and *Big Body, Tiny Head* (Short Audio Play, Royal Court Theatre). Alongside writing, Sarah works as Director of Talent at the music-tech start up, ROLI in Dalston, London.

Elizabeth Kwenortey is a screenwriter and playwright. In 2018 her play *Soon in the 4ciable Future* was commissioned and produced for Little Pieces of Gold's 'Other Loves in Crisis' Festival at the Canal Café Theatre in London. As a new writer, Elizabeth has sought to create pieces that explore various topics of interest and experience, including class, the transition from childhood to adulthood and significant moments in global history. Elizabeth recently made her directorial debut with the direction of her screenplay, *M!lking L!ons* which premiered in March 2019 for fellow students at The University of Edinburgh. She continues to write for both stage and screen, and is keen to explore, collaborate and develop further as a writer.

Clare Joy Langford is an actress and writer from Ireland. She began penning original scripts and adapting screenplays for stage while a member of her University Drama Society. During her time on the acting pathway at Drama Centre London, Clare collaborated with the writing pathway, and developed two short films under the guidance of renowned novelist and TV writer Isabelle Grey. These were screened at the Curzon and the Ritzy in London as part of the DCL graduation showcase, and she was then commissioned to write and direct a short film for Refugee Awareness Week. She has also written and produced short films for the festival circuit and devised theatre pieces for the European City of Culture Festival, Young Vic New Voices, The Waterloo Vaults Festival, Romanian Theatre Festival, Dublin Fringe Festival and Toronto Fringe Festival. *The Petal and The Orchid* was her first co-writing venture with Gabrielle Curtis.

Joanne Lau was an award-winning stand-up comedian on the UK circuit before swapping her mic for a pen. She was selected for the BBC Writersroom Comedy Room 2015/2016 and on the BBC New Talent Hotlist 2017. She has also been a finalist for the BAFTA Rocliffe New Writing Forum for TV

Drama, Royal Court Theatre and Kudos Writing Fellowship, Felix Dexter Bursary, Canneseries In Development, Cinequest Teleplay 60, Sitcom Mission, Funny Women Comedy Writing Awards and ArtsEd New Writing Project. Her credits have included Radio 4's Sketchtopia, CBBC's Class Dismissed and Cbeebies' Kit and Pup. When she is not writing, Joanne is a neuroscience technician in a brain tumour research lab.

Jasmin Mandi-Ghomi is a British-Iranian playwright who trained at both the Central School of Speech and Drama and Queen Mary University of London. Her most recent play is *Allah in the Walls*, which she wrote as part of a two-week writing residency with the North Wall Arts Centre in Oxford and which she previewed at the theatre's Alchymy Festival. At the start of 2019, Jasmin worked with Anima Theatre Company for a collaborative piece staged at the Arcola Theatre called *Where We Are: The Mosque*. It revolved around four different Islamic characters and Jasmin wrote this alongside four different playwrights. Jasmin has also been working on a series of one-woman plays with her theatre company Storm The Gods. The first of these was *Maddy*, a modern retelling of the Greek tragedy *Medea*. It was staged in London at both the Drayton Arms Theatre and the Bread and Roses Theatre.

Katherine Manners is an emerging UK playwright. Her short play *Don't Cross Bridges* was first performed at St James' Theatre and then commissioned and produced by Little Pieces of Gold at Southwark Playhouse. Her short play *Lucky George* was performed at the RADA studios and the London Transport Museum. *Goodbye Rosetta* was performed at Brighton, Camden and Edinburgh fringe festivals in 2018; Katherine also co-wrote *Marlene – The Competition* with dancer Eva Magyar which toured internationally. Her new play *The Kettling* is due to open in Brighton in 2020.

Jaki McCarrick is an award-winning writer of plays, poetry and fiction. Her play *Leopoldville* won the 2010 Papatango Prize for New Writing, and her most recent play, *The Naturalists*, premiered last year in New York to rave reviews, staged by The Pond Theatre Company at Soho Repertory Theatre, New York. Her play *Belfast Girls* was developed at the National Theatre Studio, London, and was shortlisted for the 2012 Susan Smith Blackburn Prize and the 2014 BBC Tony Doyle Award. It premiered in the US in Chicago in 2015 to much critical acclaim and has since been staged widely internationally and premiered in Australia and Sweden in 2019. In 2016, Jaki was selected for Screen Ireland's Talent Development Initiative and has recently completed the screen adaptation of *Belfast Girls*. Jaki's short story 'The Visit' won the 2010 Wasafiri Short Fiction Prize and her story collection *The Scattering* was published by Seren Books and was shortlisted for the 2014 Edge Hill Prize. Jaki, who was longlisted in 2014 for the inaugural Irish Fiction Laureate, is currently editing her first novel.

Morgan Lloyd Malcolm is a playwright and screenwriter. Her play *Emilia* transferred to the Vaudeville Theatre after a sell-out run at Shakespeare's

Globe in August 2018. Her play *Belongings* was produced at the Hampstead Theatre and Trafalgar Studios in 2011 to great acclaim and was shortlisted for The Charles Wintour Most Promising Playwright Award. This was followed in 2015 by *The Wasp* at Hampstead Theatre which also transferred to Trafalgar Studios in 2015. Other stage work includes commissions for the Old Vic, Clean Break and Firehouse Productions. In 2013 she was chosen as a member of Soho Six (Soho Theatre). She has co-written several acclaimed immersive site specific plays with Katie Lyons, produced by Look Left Look Right, including *You Once Said Yes*, *Above and Beyond*, and *Once Upon a Christmas*. She was part of the writing team for four of the Lyric Hammersmith's pantomimes from 2009 to 2012 and wrote (solo) the Bolton Octagon's Christmas plays for 2013 and 2014. She has written two large community plays for the Old Vic New Voices: *Platform* and *Epidemic*. She is currently under commission with Headlong and Cleanbreak. She is developing three films, including an adaption of *The Wasp*, and a television series.

Felix O'Brien is a writer, actor and theatre practitioner based on the west coast of Scotland. He trained at ALRA, and has attended invitational writers' groups at the Royal Court, Theatre503, Soho Theatre and The Tron. To date, his work has been presented at Southwark Playhouse, The Bunker, The Finborough, The King's Head, Theatre503, The Old Red Lion, Waterloo East, The Cockpit, The Charing Cross Theatre, The Old Hairdressers, Latitude Festival and Paines Plough's Roundabout at the Edinburgh Fringe, among others. He has previously made the shortlists for Channel 4's 4Screenwriting attachment programme, HighTide's First Commissions and Playwrights' Studio Scotland's New Playwright's Award.

Lydia Parker is a writer, director and actor originally from New York where she had her first plays produced: *Sonnie's Dead* at Synchronicity Theatre and *My Fifteen Minutes* at Brooklyn Arts Council. Since moving to London, Lydia's full-length plays *Gringo* and *American Dream* were produced at the Union Theatre and New Wimbledon Studio, and her short plays *A Better Pronoun* and *A Sort of Story* have both been produced by Little Pieces of Gold. She is a comedy sketch writer with her writing partner Maureen Oakeley with shows at the Hen and Chickens, Canal Café, Hard Rock Café and the Edinburgh Festival, and has written the live sitcom, *All I Need is a Fuck Buddy*. She also writes and directs the comedy musical web series, *The Band Formerly Known As*, and has written for several BBC Radio 4 comedy sketch shows: *Recorded for Training Purposes*, *Laura Solon* and *Lawrence and Gus*. As a theatre director and artistic director of Over Here Theatre Company, Lydia has directed and produced *ObamAmerica* at Theatre503, and *Our American Cousin* and *Dolphins and Sharks* at the Finborough Theatre. Her production of *The Actor's Nightmare* by Tony award-winning American playwright Christopher Durang was presented at the Park Theatre in July 2019. She teaches playwriting at the Actors Centre London and Writing West Midlands.

Christine Robertson featured on the BBC's New Talent Hot List 2017, and her screen credits include *Trollied*, *The Dumping Ground* and *Andy & The Odd Socks*. Her short play *Stopcock* was commissioned and produced for Little Pieces of Gold at Southwark Playhouse, and also showed at Clapham's Omnibus Theatre and the Canal Café Theatre. A full-length version is in development.

Corinne Salisbury is a playwright based in Edinburgh. She was one of the 2016 winners of the Playwrights' Studio Scotland New Playwrights Award, for which she was mentored by Zinnie Harris and Philip Howard. While based in London she had work performed at venues including Hampstead Theatre, Theatre503, the Old Red Lion, the Spiegeltent, Live Theatre Newcastle, Camden People's Theatre, the Yard Theatre, the Old Vic, and at the Public Theater in New York. Since moving to Scotland in 2015 she has been longlisted for the Tron Theatre's Progressive Playwright competition and for the Tron's Mayfesto commission 2019; had short plays performed with the Mixtape new musical theatre project, at the CCA in Glasgow, with Village Pub Theatre and Hidden Door Festival in Edinburgh, and on Tron Theatre main stage; and was commissioned to write two new full-length plays for Strange Town youth theatre, performed at the Scottish Storytelling Centre and the Traverse Theatre. She is a current recipient of an Athenaeum Award from the Royal Conservatoire of Scotland, for a creative research project to write a new play that brings a fresh approach to literary biography. Her work is also supported by the Peggy Ramsay Foundation.

Daisy Stenham is a playwright and screenwriter. She has had work performed at Southwark Playhouse, Theatre N16, Theatre Deli and The Brockley Jack Theatre. She has written and directed three short films, the first of which won Best Short Film at The London Independent Film Festival 2017. *Skin*, her latest short film, was commission by the BBC and BFI as a part of their Born Digital series, marking the thirtieth anniversary of the World Wide Web in March 2019.

Foreword

Morgan Lloyd Malcolm

When I was in sixth form studying for my A Levels and looking for performance pieces for my exams I struggled hugely with finding anything really meaty and interesting to perform as a young woman. Part of the issue was that the availability of play texts wasn't what they are now and I was working with a limited canon from the school library of the 'Classics', and besides *Saint Joan* by Bernard Shaw and a bit of Shakespeare I remember thinking to myself 'is this it?' In the end my friend and I decided to do Pinter's *Dumb Waiter* and simply drag up as men. We had a lot of fun because they are fun parts to play but I do recall the sense that only men get to do these kinds of roles.

It has always stayed with me and when I started to have my initial ideas for my play *The Wasp* I very much wanted to write a play for women to perform that was funny and dark and layered, and which would give two actresses something to really get their teeth into. When I decided to write my play *Emilia* for an all-female cast it was, again, a conscious decision not least to give more actresses jobs; it was also a play that needed to be told from a woman's perspective, including the male characters. The appetite for these plays among actresses ever since has been wonderful to see but also a real indication of just how starved we all are of fantastic plays told from a woman's perspective and performed by women.

There has recently been a real appetite for plays that present the female perspective but also show true representation on stage for women from all walks of life. It feels like we are in the midst of change and all of us at the centre of it are looking back at previous pushes and hoping that this time the change will stick. We are constantly told that all the stories have been told and that we are simply retelling them again and again. I would suggest that all of a certain kind of story has been told by one small section of our world's population – it's time to let the rest of us tell our stories.

I don't know about you but I want to read and see stories by women. I want to read stories by Black and Asian writers. By D/deaf writers. By disabled writers. By blind or visually impaired writers. Trans and non-binary writers. European writers. Working-class writers and writers from disadvantaged socio-economic circumstances. This list goes on and on. I want to read and see work that doesn't need the writer to be considered the 'author' but rather a member of a large creative team working towards a beautiful collaboration that has no hierarchies in the traditional sense. I want us to recognise how dependent on the patriarchy and capitalism the theatre industry is and start working towards dismantling and rebuilding it. I want our beautiful industry to be for all and not just for some. Theatre should be for everyone – whether that's who is being employed to make it or who is able to afford to see it.

This collection of plays is an important part of this wave of change. It's heartening and exciting to know that this book will form a resource for schools, universities and theatre companies – professional or otherwise – to perform. It is work like this that will move the need for change forward. Because there is only so much that talking can achieve and really we need to get on with doing it. So I hope in borrowing or purchasing this book you feel compelled to be part of this action. That you feel emboldened by it and that with each performance of one of these brilliant plays we manage to step even closer to a theatrical landscape that better represents the world we see around us and that this will truly benefit us all.

Morgan Lloyd Malcolm
April 2019

Acknowledgements

I want to thank Leigh and Rebecca who always encourage and support.
I would like to mention all the playwrights who continue to inspire me.
I want to acknowledge my editor Ben Piggott, who agreed without hesitation with the need for this book.

Professional performing rights

Publication of these plays does not indicate their availability for professional performance, and applications for professional performances should be made before rehearsals begin. Applications for performance by professionals in any medium through the world should be addressed to the following:

Alive Day   Knight Hall Agency Ltd, Lower Ground Floor, 7 Mallow Street, London EC1Y 8RQ. Email: office@knighthallagency.com

A Better Pronoun   Email: Lydia.parker@btinternet.com

A Prince   Email: dbetti@outlook.com

Coconut Diaries   Email: stellaajayi14@gmail.com

Come Die With Me   Email: vicki.connerty@googlemail.com

Consolea   Email: laura.jayne.ayres.writing@gmail.com

Copycat   Berlin Associates, 7 Tyers Gate, London SE1 3HX. Email: agents@berlinassociates.com

Do You Pray?   Email: alexrusher@independenttalent.com

Don't Cross Bridges   Email: kathmanners@googlemail.com

Echoes Through the Dust   Kitson Press Associates, 32 Tavistock Street, London WC2E 7PB. Email: info@kitsonpress.co.uk

Fox   The Agency, 24 Pottery Lane, London W11 4LZ. Email: info@theagency.co.uk

Girlboss   Email: corinne_s@hotmail.co.uk

Hurricane Blues   Curtis Brown Haymarket House, 28–29 Haymarket, London SW1Y 4SP

Love By Numbers   Blake Friedmann Literary Agency Ltd, Ground Floor, 15 Highbury Place, London N5 1QP. Email: louisa@blakefriedmann.co.uk

Of Things Unsaid   Email: j.mandi.ghomi@gmail.com

Soon In the 4ciable Future   Email: elizabeth.kwenortey@gmail.com

Swipe   Email: gracecarroll06@gmail.com

The Petal and The Orchid   Email: gabzcurtis@gmail.com clare.joy.langford@gmail.com

The Pillory   Email: adamfelixobrien@gmail.com

Stopcock   Curtis Brown Literary Agents, Haymarket House, 28–29 Haymarket, London SW1Y 4SP

Two Sisters   Curtis Brown Literary Agents, Haymarket House, 28–29 Haymarket, London SW1Y 4SP. Email: www.permissions.curtisbrown.co.uk

Tussy   Email: jaki_mac@hotmail.com

Introduction

The thing that excites me about theatre is the chance to study human behaviour, to watch ourselves in all our glorious complexity. Except for a long time we weren't watching everyone equally; historically, women have been under-represented on stage and it has only been over the past few years that we have started to see a shift. But the lack of women's roles over the years has reduced the choice of suitable play texts available for training; it has led to casting anomalies in final drama school showcases where you frequently see four women playing one central role, with each woman handing the role on like a baton in a relay, and in youth theatre productions where there are already fewer male students so that girls double up or take on boys' roles. It's not just about quantity but quality too. Women's roles are still frequently less challenging, less likely to drive the story and only suitable for actresses from a narrower range of ages and backgrounds. Unsurprisingly, aspiring actors are fed up. They want complex roles that are integral to the play, develop their training, skills and confidence, and which truly represent the lives of all women.

This anthology is an antidote to the limited and limiting range of theatre roles for women by offering twenty-two contemporary short plays in which women drive the action. The collection offers intelligent, emotionally nuanced roles and a wide choice of acting styles for actors of different ages and backgrounds. Students will benefit from having a complete text in which all the playwright's intentions, creativity and conclusions are in evidence and can enjoy stories and scenarios that offer their characters a full journey, with an emotional arc that can be followed through from beginning to end. With afterwords from the playwrights and details about the original productions, the collection is a perfect resource for aspiring actors whether they be in university, drama school or theatre groups.

All the plays in the anthology were developed and produced since 2010 for Little Pieces of Gold. It is a record of what our playwrights are thinking and writing about now, covering a broad range of themes, including among others the me-too movement, identity politics, class, relationships, university life and the impact of social media. Little Pieces of Gold is a theatre company renowned for championing new writing. It is committed to equal representation of both actors and writers, and the script selection process encourages this by operating a widely publicised open submission call that receives almost 3,000 short plays a year. This means that people from all walks of life, those without access to the theatre industry, or those who have not had the privilege of a university or drama school training, get the opportunity to have their writing produced. It also means that our playwrights are writing roles that resonate deeply with a wide cross-section of women today; *Short Plays with Great Roles for Women* does just that.

Suzette Coon
May 2019

Part I

Crossing bridges

1 *Two Sisters*

Fiona Doyle

Characters

NORAH, *early forties, caustic at times.*
NIAMH, *mid-thirties, a little naive.*
AUNTY MARY, *late sixties. Estranged sister of Niamh and Norah's father.*

Notes

Niamh and Norah have been responsible for the care of their elderly father for the past ten years. They live in an old cottage in rural Northern Ireland (though this setting can be altered depending on the actors' needs).
(/) marks the point where the immediately following dialogue interrupts.
(–) marks an abrupt cut-off.
(Beat) indicates a brief break in the dialogue.
(Pause) indicates where there is a thought process happening.
(Silence) indicates the point at which characters do not know what to say next, or how to say it.
(…) indicates where speech trails off.

Original production details

Two Sisters was commissioned and produced by Little Pieces of Gold at Southwark Playhouse on 24 November 2013.

The cast was as follows:

AUNTY MARY	Jo Cooklin
NORAH	Claire Garrigan
NIAMH	Fiona McKinnon
Director:	Rebecca Hill

Scene One

Darkness. Niamh is already in bed. Norah is just getting into bed. Silence. Then hushed voices.

NIAMH: NORAH?
NORAH: What?
NIAMH: Can ya hear that?
NORAH: What?
NIAMH: I think … I think it's snow.

Pause.

NORAH: You can't hear snow.
NIAMH: Oh.
NORAH: Go back to sleep.

Pause.

NIAMH: NORAH?
NORAH: What?
NIAMH: How was he?
NORAH: Fine.
NIAMH: Fine?
NORAH: Fine.
NIAMH: Right. (Beat) You sure he was fine now?
NORAH: Yeah.
NIAMH: Right. (Pause) Nor/ah?
NORAH: What?
NIAMH: He was on about Aunty Mary earlier.
NORAH: What?
NIAMH: In his sleep.

Pause.

NORAH: Strange.
NIAMH: Yeah.
NORAH: They've not spoken in years.
NIAMH: Yeah.

Pause.

NORAH: Must be all the drugs.

Pause.

NIAMH: I'm tired.
NORAH: Go to sleep then!

Pause.

NIAMH: Cold in here. (Beat) Smells of damp. (Beat) Some sun would be nice. (Beat) An' some sea. (Beat) An' a nice jam sandwich. (Pause) Norah? (Pause) Norah? (Pause) Night then.

Silence.

Scene Two

Next morning. Norah and Niamh sit at kitchen table. Their elderly, dying father lies in a room offstage. Norah has a list and is sorting medication into a little pill box. A dressing robe hangs on the back of her chair. Niamh sits and watches her. Both sisters are unfashionably dressed in lots of warm layers. Niamh eventually exits to father's room offstage. Norah continues sorting. After a while Niamh re-enters and sits.

NIAMH: I don't think he'll last long.
NORAH: You said that last year.

Pause.

NIAMH: This place is a dump.
NORAH: What?
NIAMH: Look at that wall there. Right state. An' don't even get me started on the damp.

Norah stops sorting momentarily, looks at wall.

NORAH: D'you remember when we were wee things an' I was chasin' you? An' you were runnin' mad all round the place? An' you ran an' ya ran an' ya ran, an' then next thing, (Laughs) next thing ya ran straight into it an' split yer head open.

Pause.

NIAMH: I'll go see if he wants those curtains opened.

Niamh exits and we hear the following offstage as Norah continues sorting.

NIAMH: (Offstage) Do ya want those curtains open now? (Beat) I think I should open them. Nice day. Bright. Cold but bright. Are you cold? (Beat) I'm cold. It's cold in here. I'll get yer robe.

Niamh re-enters, fetches robe from the back of Norah's chair.

NORAH: An' ya had to have three, no, four, ya had to have four stitches in an' you screamed like a mini-banshee, d'you remember?

Niamh has exited again.

NIAMH: (Offstage) There. Better now. Don't ya think? (Beat) I think it might snow. (Pause) Right then.

Niamh re-enters.

NORAH: An' da used call you 'stitches,' d'you remember? He used say things like 'where's stitches got to?' or 'tell stitches her dinner's ready,' or 'quiet stitches, the news is – '
NIAMH: Alright, alright! I know how the story goes.

Pause. Norah pushes pill box towards Niamh and calls out the names of the drugs from a piece of paper while Niamh checks they're in the pill box. It's a well-rehearsed, familiar routine.

NORAH: Bethnelan.
NIAMH: Yeah.
NORAH: 2 GTN Sublingual.
NIAMH: Yeah.
NORAH: 2 Ditropan.
NIAMH: Yeah.
NORAH: 2 Repaglimide.
NIAMH: Yeah.
NORAH: 1 Co-dydramol.
NIAMH: Yeah.
NORAH: 1 Metformin.
NIAMH: Yeah.
NORAH: 2 Zestril.
NIAMH: Yeah.
NORAH: 2 Simvastatin.
NIAMH: Yeah.
NORAH: 1 Loprazolan.
NIAMH: Yeah.
BOTH: 1 Paroxetine.

Beat.

NIAMH: Yeah.
NORAH: Right. (Beat) That's him set up for the day then.

Scene Three

Evening. Two weeks later. Empty kitchen. Norah and Niamh, along with Aunty Mary, enter. All dressed in funeral attire. Niamh and Aunty Mary sit. Aunty

Mary in same chair as Norah in the previous scene. Norah remains standing.
It's cold. Norah and Aunty Mary leave their coats on. Niamh unbuttons her coat
but does not take it off.

AUNTY MARY: Small turn out.
NORAH: Yeah.
NIAMH: Not big at all.

Silence.

AUNTY MARY: The priest said some nice things.
NORAH: He did.
NIAMH: Oh he did.

Silence.

NIAMH: Thanks for comin' all this way Aunty Mary.
AUNTY MARY: Well, it's been too long now. I was always so fond of you both.
NIAMH: Must've been a shock.
AUNTY MARY: In a way. (Beat) But ... I think I knew. Felt it. In my bones. An'
    my tummy. Had a funny feelin' in my tummy that mornin'. I could ... it
    was in the air all round me. An' then it started to snow. When the phone
    rang that is. It started to snow when the phone rang. Big soft flakes floatin'
    down. Big soft ones. An' all the street noise went quiet. An' I knew then.
    (Pause) That wall's a right state! Place could do with a lick of paint,
    couldn't it? Mind you, he was never a house-proud man my brother, god
    rest his soul.

Pause.

NIAMH: I was thinkin' yellow.
NORAH: What?
NIAMH: Yellow. Paint. I've always fancied a yellow kitchen.
NORAH: Have ya now.
AUNTY MARY: Yellow?
NIAMH: I like canaries.
AUNTY MARY: I'm not so sure. Fer a kitchen? No, I'd think more along the lines
    of a smart beige or a nice cream if I were you.
NIAMH: Cream.
AUNTY MARY: An' I could help you know.
NIAMH: Cream instead.
AUNTY MARY: I've some leftover paint you could use an' all. Make a weekend
    of it maybe? I'll bring yer cousin Ruth down. Did you know she's an inte-
    rior designer now?
NORAH: Really.

AUNTY MARY: Oh yes. A real flair for it she has. Keep tellin' her she should try her luck on that Changin' Rooms show. D'you watch it?

NORAH: No.

NIAMH: An' she'd come/all this way?

NORAH: Do they even make/it anymore?

AUNTY MARY: Oh she loves a challenge/my Ruthie does.

NORAH: An' it's all a bit soon/don't ye think?

NIAMH: That's so kind've ya Aunty Mary. Thank/you so much.

AUNTY MARY: No need to thank me at all luvvie. It/would –

NORAH: You can't paint the place over. You can't just … fuckin' paint the place over!

Silence.

AUNTY MARY: Bit cold in here.

NIAMH: (To Norah) Why not?

AUNTY MARY: (To herself) Is that damp/I smell?

NORAH: He's only just dead! Fresh in the ground! So stop it! Both of ye. Ye've no right at all to be carryin' on this way.

Pause. It starts to rain.

NIAMH: Right.

Silence.

NIAMH: Will ya have some tea?

AUNTY MARY: Ah no. No, it's late an' I'd not meant to stop so long. (Niamh glares at Norah. Aunty Mary stands.) Now, you know where I am.

NIAMH: Yes. We do. We do now.

AUNTY MARY: Call whenever you want.

NIAMH: Yes.

AUNTY MARY: Don't be strangers.

NIAMH: We will. Call, I mean. We'll have more time now.

AUNTY MARY: We'll take a walk on the beach. Ye've not been there since ye were wee ones. D'ye remember? We'd take picnics. All've us adults and you kiddies, all together before … oh you used both love the sea. An' the sand. An' a nice jam sandwich. D'you know, I was worried I might not recognise you both.

NORAH: We'll be in touch.

Niamh escorts Aunty Mary out. Re-enters and both sisters sit. Norah sits in Aunty Mary's chair.

NORAH: Can see why they never spoke –

NIAMH: You were so rude. Like a/child you were.

NORAH: Don't need to paint that wall. Fine the way/it is. She's just interferin'.

NIAMH: I'd like to take a walk on the beach. I remember that beach. We had fun there.

Pause.
It is still raining.

NIAMH: Let's go out.

NORAH: Where?

NIAMH: I don't know. Anywhere! To a pub. For a drink. A night out.

NORAH: Now?

NIAMH: Yes.

NORAH: No.

NIAMH: No?

NORAH: No. We need to … be here. That's what we need to do now. That's all we need to do now.

Pause.
Then Niamh stands up abruptly, buttoning her coat. She heads for the door.

NORAH: Where are ya –

NIAMH: (Turns abruptly and faces her sister.) HAVE YOU SEEN THE STATE OF THAT WALL? No care. Left to rot. An' this whole place smells of damp an' I'm sick of it I am! Sick of breathin' it in all day long. I'm tired of it. I'm tired. I want … I want it to start.

Niamh leaves. Norah goes to follow but stops at door. Turns and looks at room. Walks slowly to chair, and considers removing her coat. She hovers there, looking back and forth between her father's room and the door her sister has just walked through. Silence. Sound of rain.

Ends.

Afterword

Fiona Doyle

In *Two Sisters* we never meet the father, but his shadow still permeates the piece. Whether they realise it or not (and I think ultimately that must be the individual actor's decision) Niamh and Norah have inherited a kind of trauma from their father. We don't ever understand the details of this trauma, but we have a sense that it exists.

Before his death the sisters are tied to their filial duty; their lives dictated by a dying man's needs. When Niamh points out that the wall is mouldy, leading

Norah to recall the time her younger sister ran into it and needed stitches, the wall becomes more than just a wall. It becomes symbolic of the kind of relationship these women had with their father; one that has damaged them physically and emotionally. Perhaps Norah's recollection of how Niamh acquired her injury isn't even accurate. Perhaps she has replaced a traumatic and more sinister memory with one that is easier to digest and cope with later in life.

After his death there is still no release. With the arrival of their estranged aunt we begin to wonder if perhaps they can start rebuilding their lives, as well as their relationships with themselves and with others. But it quickly becomes apparent that it won't be as easy as that. The line 'You can't just … fuckin' paint the place over!' is indicative of this in the sense that it takes a long time to recover from a lifetime of trauma and damaging behaviour. They both have an uphill struggle ahead.

But I think ultimately we are left with a glimmer of hope. At the end of the play Niamh leaves. She walks out; refusing to be damaged any further. And in walking out, she leaves Norah with a choice to make – will she remain where she is, both physically and psychologically? Or will she follow her sister's lead and, in doing so, break a suffocating, negative cycle once and for all? So the play ends hovering on a decision that has yet to be made; nothing is neatly resolved, but everything is left to play for.

2 *A Prince*

Dipo Baruwa-Etti

Characters

WONU, *female, forties, Nigerian.*
SOLA, *female, forties, Nigerian.*

Notes

(–) on its own marks a pause. Each of these can last as long as [and be filled however] the director chooses.
(–) at the end of a line indicates being cut off.
(/) marks the point where the immediately following dialogue interrupts.
(…) at the end of a speech means it trails off.
Dialogue in italics is Yoruba words/phrases.

Original production details

A Prince was commissioned and produced by Little Pieces of Gold at Southwark Playhouse on 24 September 2017.

The cast was as follows:

SOLA	Sabrina Richmond
WONU	Chiedza Rwodzi
Director:	Gemma Aked-Priestly

Nigeria, present day. Sola cleans her sitting room with a broom. In front of her are mason jars, each with a different substance – water, blood, powder, etc. Wonu storms inside.

WONU: Sola, I need your help.
SOLA: Can't you see that I'm busy?
WONU: It's urgent.
SOLA: I'm busy.
WONU: Sola, please.

–

SOLA: What is it, jo?
WONU: I need your help.
SOLA: You said that.

—

—

SOLA: What have you done? Wonu?
WONU: It's not what I've done. It's what he's done.
SOLA: Who?
WONU: Who do you think?
SOLA: So you come to me?
WONU: I need your help.
SOLA: What happened to being a good Christian girl?
WONU: I am.
SOLA: I thought good Christian girls didn't resort to juju?
WONU: I'm desperate.
SOLA: I thought juju was an abomination.
WONU: It is.
SOLA: Yet you come to me.
WONU: I didn't say it was for juju, did I?

—

SOLA: So?

—

SOLA: I thought so.... So what is it?
WONU: I ...
SOLA: You ...
WONU: I ...
SOLA: You ...
WONU: I ...
SOLA: Sister, speak.
WONU: She's pregnant.
SOLA: Tokumbo?
WONU: No.
SOLA: Then/who?
WONU: The new one.
SOLA: He has a new one?
WONU: Went to Ilesha for work, a few months ago. Came back one week later
  with a new girl. They arrived when I was burying my baby. As I threw the
  last bit of dirt, I heard the laughter. Another week later, they married.
SOLA: Wife number three.

WONU: I stood there, tears still fresh.

SOLA: He's collecting them, eh?

WONU: As this baby marries the man that I first loved fifteen years ago.

SOLA: The man that you never gave children.

WONU: Children are easy to give. Tokumbo gave him children. Four children. But children are not enough. We all know that. He needs an heir. He needs a prince.

SOLA: We already tried getting you pregnant.

WONU: I know.

SOLA: The curse is too strong.

WONU: You said.

SOLA: The power of our forefathers too resilient.

WONU: Yes.

SOLA: So what are you doing here?

WONU: I told you, she's pregnant. I've tried to be strong for months, brush it aside, but …

—

SOLA: I'm not going to tell you what to do.

WONU: Sola –

SOLA: If you come into my house, you need to have solutions. Ask and you shall be given. You understand those words, eh?

WONU: Yes.

SOLA: So?

WONU: I …

SOLA: The sun is going down.

WONU: I know. I …

SOLA: Tick tock, tick tock … (sighs, fed up) Do you want her to have a girl?

WONU: It's too late.

SOLA: It's never too late.

WONU: The doctor has said.

SOLA: Doctors make mistakes.

WONU: They'll know someone interfered.

SOLA: They won't.

WONU: The Lord will reveal.

SOLA: *Kin o nfe*, Wonu?

WONU: I …

SOLA: You're here now. Stop doing *shakara*.

WONU: I'm not.

SOLA: Acting like the good little Christian girl. You've been here before, and you'll be here again.

WONU: I won't.

SOLA: Should I kill it?

WONU: I …

SOLA: Wonu!

WONU: Let him live.

SOLA: What?

WONU: Let him live, and let him have a prince.

SOLA: Why are you here then?

WONU: But make that prince a peasant.

SOLA: Now, we're/talking.

WONU: Make sure that he grows to be a good man. A handsome man.

SOLA: *Kini –*

WONU: But a failure.

SOLA: Ah.

WONU: He'll be highly educated, but he'll never find work. It'll break him. He'll cry out to the Lord. Everything he touches will vanish. Like Job, but no restoration.

SOLA: Are you sure?

WONU: Am/I sure?

SOLA: This is worse than death.

WONU: Do you know what else is worse than death? Barrenness.

SOLA: It doesn't have to be.

WONU: It's all he sees when he looks at me.

SOLA: I don't think –

WONU: The wife who has littered the fields with dead babies. Babies that have never seen the light of day. A cemetery of twelve.

SOLA: W/onu.

WONU: With their little crosses. What did I do to deserve that?

SOLA: You don't.

WONU: Exactly. I'm a good person. I honoured my mother and my father, I went to university, I fell in love, I married, I was the perfect housewife. Not a day went by without food on that table. Even when the lights went off, I had food on that table. I never spoke against him. I respected him. I washed his feet. On my hands and knees. I worship him and he makes me feel like I'm nothing. But he'll learn that a prince does not make perfect.

SOLA: Are you sure you want to do this?

WONU: When did you start thinking about morals?

SOLA: I'm not. I'm thinking of you.

WONU: Don't worry about me. This will bring me joy.

SOLA: You could be dead before he's even old.

WONU: I won't be.

SOLA: You can kill him.

WONU: You've gone soft.

SOLA: No.

WONU: Did my words hit home last time?

SOLA: No, I –

WONU: Then do as I ask.

SOLA: Wonu.

WONU: Do you know how it feels? How humiliating it is?

SOLA: You can leave.

WONU: You act like you don't know this land. Where shall I go? If I walk to the waters, who will be by my side?

SOLA: Go out west.

WONU: This is my home.

SOLA: Wonu.

WONU: You wouldn't understand.

SOLA: *Ọmọ mi ti kú*, Wonu. *Meji.* You're not the only one.

WONU: But you still have one. You still have a prince.

SOLA: Even if I didn't –

WONU: Sola, are you gonna do this or not?

–

SOLA: Do you have a relic?

Wonu reaches into her pocket and brings out a sonogram. She hands it to Sola.

SOLA: Won't they know it's missing.

WONU: It's a copy.

SOLA: Now, *kunle.*

WONU: Me?

SOLA: Yes.

WONU: Why?

SOLA: Because I said so.

WONU: I've never had to do that before.

SOLA: I want you to beg.

WONU: Beg?

SOLA: Ask for forgiveness.

WONU: I won't.

SOLA: Then you better find another doctor to do this for you. Try and find one as discreet as me.

WONU: Sola.

SOLA: Beg.

WONU: Sola.

SOLA: *Kunle.*

–

–

SOLA: How badly do you want him destroyed?

–

SOLA: *Kunle.*

Wonu goes down on her knees.

SOLA: Say sorry.
WONU: Sorry.
SOLA: Properly.
WONU: Sola, I'm sorry.
SOLA: No. Denounce him. Denounce your maker.
WONU: Never.
SOLA: Do it.
WONU: I love Him.
SOLA: He won't want you after this. Trust me. It's bigger than anything.
WONU: Why don't we try and make me pregnant again?
SOLA: It's too much.
WONU: We can do it.
SOLA: You had to go to hospital last time.
WONU: I'm stronger now.
SOLA: Denounce Him.
WONU: Sola, please. Have mercy.

Sola hands Wonu the sonogram. Wonu doesn't take it and kneels back down.

WONU: You have forsaken me, Lord. Now I forsake you.

—

SOLA: Now, we begin.

Sola puts the sonogram into a large bowl. She pours blood on it.

SOLA: Are you not going to watch?

Wonu shakes her head. Sola continues. She pours some powder into it, closes her eyes, and hovers her hand over the bowl, whispering a prayer to herself. Despite herself, Wonu steals a quick glance, but then she turns away.

SOLA: You know, this is actually fun … I rarely destroy futures in this manner.
WONU: Just do your best.
SOLA: Oh, don't you worry about that.

Sola takes out the sonogram and hangs it on a drying line.

SOLA: Are you sure you want to do this?

Wonu looks Sola in the eye. She puts a hand on her stomach, and nods frantically.

SOLA: Okay. I'll take it to 3am prayer.

Wonu nods.
Sola approaches her and extends her hand.

SOLA: It was good seeing you again, my sister.

Wonu nods. She takes a bill out of her pocket and hands it to Sola.

SOLA: My hands are dirty. Just put it down.

Wonu puts the money on the floor.

SOLA: You should join us again.

Wonu shakes her head.

SOLA: I'm going to clean up. I hope you change your mind.

Sola exits. We hear the sound of water running.
Wonu stares at the sonogram and takes a deep breath.

Ends.

Afterword

Dipo Baruwa-Etti

A Prince tells the story of a woman who visits a witch doctor in order to curse her husband's unborn son. I wrote this play because I wanted to explore a practice that is still common in Africa (witchcraft) but in a way that felt grounded and honest – not so mystical. I also wanted to explore a world in which polygamy is still prevalent, as is the idea that sons are more important than daughters. It was interesting to think about how all these factors could collide and cause drama.

Naturally, when thinking about people who visit witch doctors in order to curse others, we picture them as villainous. With *A Prince* I wanted to turn the tables. What if the woman seeking a curse wasn't an evil stepmother? What if her ask came out of desperation and sadness? What if the patriarchy had battered her so much that she takes it out not on the present system but on the future one? And with the witch doctor character, I desired to question what actions could challenge one's moral compass. Is an unborn child fair game or does that bring an existential dilemma?

These ideas and questions were a catalyst for this play's existence and it was exciting to write two African women who were neither black nor white. Whose encounter would not only force them to confront their ideology, but force an audience to. Force me to.

3   *Do You Pray?*

Yasmin Joseph

Characters

EVELYN, *an elder Caribbean woman, knowing, assured.*
NADINE, *twenties, a Black British woman, observant, attentive.*

Notes

(–) at the end of a line indicates being cut off.
(…) indicates where speech trails off.
(Beat) indicates a brief break in the dialogue.
(Pause) indicates where there is a thought process happening.

Original production details

Do You Pray? was first commissioned by Rapid Write Response at Theatre503 and then produced by Little Pieces of Gold at Southwark Playhouse on 4 February 2018.

The cast was as follows:

EVELYN	Michelle Greenidge
NADINE	Nicole Sawyyer
Director:	Rebekah Murrell

Present day. A living room, with all of the crochet, plastic flowers and royal para-phernalia that indicate a Caribbean grandmother's home. A long wilful silence, toe tapping, tea stirring. Evelyn basks in it, whilst Nadine struggles to stay afloat.

EVELYN: (Finally) Your brother got married.
NADINE: I saw.
EVELYN: You did?
NADINE: Facebook.
EVELYN: Of course.

Pause.

NADINE: I liked your dress. I hadn't seen you dress up like that in years. I was shocked.

EVELYN: Well it was a special occasion.

Beat.

NADINE: You were beaming. And the cake? Who made that cake? It was huge.

EVELYN: Your Aunt made it.

NADINE: She did? God I forget how good she is. In one picture it looked the same height as Uncle Ross, I was scared it was gonna topple over. Silly I know, being scared through a screen. It was just so tall and intricate.

EVELYN: You come from a family of many talents.

Beat.

NADINE: You must have loved all of the pictures. I saw all of them, Sam posted a whole album.

EVELYN: Well you know I don't keep up with those things.

NADINE: His wife looked really beautiful.

EVELYN: She's a Christian.

NADINE: That explains it.

Pause. Nadine rests her teacup and adjusts.

NADINE: I sent a card on your birthday –

Evelyn indicates towards the mantelpiece.

NADINE: The vouchers, did you get to use them?

EVELYN: When have you ever known me to like fuss?

NADINE: It's not fuss Nan, it's a birthday present.

EVELYN: Spas and things like that. When have you ever known me to do things like that? I'm a simple woman.

NADINE: Well it wasn't meant to offend you.

Pause.

EVELYN: How have you been?

NADINE: Better.

EVELYN: How have you been inside?

NADINE: (After a moment's thought) Peaceful.

EVELYN: You sure?

NADINE: I think so.

Beat.

EVELYN: You hungry?

NADINE: Not especially.

EVELYN: You want to eat?

NADINE: I'm fine.

EVELYN: I can look in your eyes and see you're not full.

Pause.

NADINE: I'll have something small.

EVELYN: You're wasting away.

NADINE: Something big then.

EVELYN: Don't get smart with me pickney.

NADINE: You know I can leave if you'd like? If that'd make this all easier.

EVELYN: Easy? Who told you this was easy? All these years in this world and not one of them was easy. So do me a favour and check easy in at the door when you come into this house. Don't insult me. Easy is fast livin –

NADINE: Here we go.

EVELYN: Easy is soulless –

NADINE: I have a soul.

EVELYN: Easy is fast money.

NADINE: I didn't come here for cheap shots.

Nadine goes to exit.

EVELYN: Run. It's all you know to do. Just like your mother.

NADINE: And stay for what? More put downs? To be made to feel worthless.

EVELYN: I'm sorry I don't have the money to make you feel worth as much as they do.

NADINE: God forgive you.

EVELYN: I read my bible.

NADINE: Yeah and what good is it doing? All that love for a white man in the sky you've never met and nothing left for your blood.

EVELYN: You watch your mouth.

NADINE: You know there are people out there on drugs, coming home once a fortnight to steal, to lie, to sell family treasures, and you know what their doors are still open. Even if someone's gotta hide a ring or two, lock away their purse. They have people who've never turned their backs on them. And all I come here for is love. All I want is for you to love me like I'm a real person and you can't even do that.

Beat.

EVELYN: I pray for you.

NADINE: I'd rather you talk to me.

EVELYN: I can't talk to you about things I don't understand.

NADINE: You haven't tried to understand.

EVELYN: You want me, a woman who's worked since the second her hands could hold weight, to understand you selling your body?

A long pause.

NADINE: I don't sell my body.

EVELYN: You're selling your body.

NADINE: I don't sell my body. No one owns me. This isn't slavery.

EVELYN: You're selling your sex.

NADINE: I sell a service. I sell a fantasy.

EVELYN: You are selling your body.

NADINE: I'm dancing.

Beat.

EVELYN: That isn't dancing. No, that is not dancing. Not from what I hear, not from what they tell me.

NADINE: I'm dancing Nan. Nothing more. Nothing less.

Pause.

EVELYN: And you feel safe there?

NADINE: Yes ... I got more abuse working at River Island.

Beat.

EVELYN: The men don't trouble you?

NADINE: They try.

EVELYN: Well you tell them where to go!

NADINE: I do!

EVELYN: Good!

Beat.

EVELYN: And I don't suppose they have a pension scheme ... in that ... line of work?

NADINE: (Wants to laugh, thinks against it) No Nan, they don't. But I save.

EVELYN: Very reckless.

NADINE: It's really not the end of the world. I'm 26.

EVELYN: So?

NADINE: So, I have time to save for my pension.

EVELYN: "I have time." Hmph. What a luxury. It's because you don't know.

NADINE: Enlighten me.

EVELYN: It's because you have so much future ahead of you, your eyes too bright to see right now.

NADINE: I'll never understand the pride you get from suffering.

EVELYN: It's because you don't know hard work.

NADINE: Big people your age, your generation, it's like they'd rather see a woman starve than live fast and get ahead.

EVELYN: Because easy come, easy go.

NADINE: Meanwhile their sons are out there wreaking the most havoc and getting praised for it.

EVELYN: That's not true, your brother was an angel.

NADINE: He wasn't perfect and you know it.

Pause.

EVELYN: Never judge yourself by the standards of men. We set the standards, and if we set them low enough then they'll be more than happy to stoop.

NADINE: And that sounds fair to you?

EVELYN: No one said life was fair. But I can tell you I've carried the loads of men my whole life and I'm a wiser woman for it.

NADINE: Wearing struggle like a badge of honour. I just don't get it.

EVELYN: In time my dear.

Evelyn rests her hand on Nadine's knee for longer than is necessary. For a moment they're content.

NADINE: I've really missed you.

Beat.

EVELYN: I should go and soak some peas.

NADINE: No. Don't worry about all that Nan. I'm heading off.

EVELYN: Without eating? What about some cake? I think I even have a slice from the wedding. It's only right you taste it. The icing is a little stiff but the cake itself is still fresh. Let me at least wrap a piece for you to take for the road. It was so popular I was lucky to get a look in.

Evelyn readies the cake with fuss.

EVELYN: And you know your father's family are like vultures. Greedy. No pride. That good for nothing Dorris got caught with three favour bags, can you imagine? I don't even know who the rest was for, seeing as her useless husband can't seem to stay out of prison. Just a little slice, I know you don't eat big. But just for the taste. You have to taste it.... It was a blessed day. Your brother looked so ... established. To live to see a day like that. God is truly good.

NADINE: You deserve it Nan. We – I – may not always show it, but I –

EVELYN: I want you to love yourself.

Pause. Nadine takes the parcel of cake.

NADINE: I'm gonna shoot now Nan.

EVELYN: You got far to go?

NADINE: Not too far.

EVELYN: Good. Bye then.

NADINE: Bye.

Nadine goes to leave.

EVELYN: Be careful. I keep hearing about them snatching people's phones.

NADINE: I'll be on the lookout.

EVELYN: And handbags.

NADINE: Thanks.

EVELYN: You warm enough in that?

NADINE: I'll be fine.

EVELYN: You look well.

NADINE: Thanks.

EVELYN: I'll tell your brother you came by.

NADINE: He won't care.

Beat.

EVELYN: You have holy water?

NADINE: I'm sure I do somewhere.

EVELYN: You still pray?

Evelyn takes Nadine's silence as a response.

EVELYN: Well you should get going, it's getting dark.

Nadine turns to leave.

EVELYN: Nadine … I don't know where you lay your head at night. I don't know if you still have it in you to humble yourself and pray. But just promise me this … make sure that when you close your door, when you're alone in those quiet hours, make sure you can live inside your skin. Make sure the things you do to feed your body don't starve your soul.

Ends.

Afterword

Yasmin Joseph

I wrote this thinking about generational perspectives, how they influence us morally and impact our sense of self. It's a question asked in many families: what should we bring forward and what needs to be left behind?

4 Don't Cross Bridges

Katherine Manners

Characters

LUCY, *late teens/early twenties, a local girl.*
NURI, *similar age, Romany Gypsy.*

Notes

(–) at the end of a line indicates being cut off.
(…) indicates where speech trails off.
(Pause) indicates where there is a thought process happening.
(Silence) indicates the point at which characters do not know what to say next, or how to say it.

Original production details

Don't Cross Bridges was commissioned and produced by Little Pieces of Gold at Southwark Playhouse on 3 July 2016.

The cast was as follows:

NURI	Maeve O'Sullivan
LUCY	Lucy-Charlotte Couture
Director:	Katie-Ann McDonough

Scrubland, down by a railway line.
Nuri enters breathless, panting. There is what looks like blood spattered on her T shirt. Lucy runs on, also breathless. Immediately Nuri pulls out a small knife and brandishes it threateningly.

LUCY: Fucking Gyppo.

Lucy pulls a small pot of red paint out of her bag.

LUCY: Shall I finish off the job?
NURI: I'll cut your fucking face off.

LUCY: We don't want Gyppos around here.

NURI: Why don't you go back? Carry on with your yelling, chucking paint about. What's it supposed to be? Blood?

LUCY: It's a reminder –

NURI: Warning more like.

LUCY: Why did you run?

NURI: Police showed up.

LUCY: Yeah, I forgot. Gyppos don't like the police. Put the knife down.

NURI: You come near me I'll cut your face off.

LUCY: I doubt it.

NURI: Stop using that word.

LUCY: I just want to talk to you, ok? Put the knife away, Jesus.

NURI: Don't come anywhere near me.

LUCY: There is no chance of that.

Nuri puts the knife away but remains wary.

LUCY: You need to tell your dad, and your brothers and sisters, and cousins, and all the bloody rest of you to get off my dad's land. Now. Today. You go back now, and you tell them to clear off. Go somewhere else, I don't care where, but just leave.

NURI: Why did you throw paint on me?

LUCY: You got in the way! It was a protest, that wasn't my … just … tell them! Will you? To clear off?

NURI: No.

LUCY: My dad, he's worked hard all his life. He's paid his taxes, which is more than any of you have ever done. Haven't paid in a penny and expect benefits. He's had it hard! And that land, he was just about to sell it. He needs the money, without it he'll be evicted! He'll be homeless. He's 70. Does this mean anything to you? Do you care at all about anyone else?

NURI: About your dad? No. I genuinely couldn't give a fuck.

LUCY: Look. He's scared. He's heartbroken. He can't sleep. I saw him crying –

NURI: What is he, a poof?

LUCY: Don't you dare mock him after what you people have done to him.

NURI: You people?

LUCY: There's shit everywhere! Literally shit – on the grass, bits of toilet roll, thick with litter, nappies, old tires. He had a heart attack last year, this is too much for him. He's vulnerable, he's on his own. This will kill him.

Pause.

LUCY: What's that smell?

NURI: What?

LUCY: Is that lavender? Why on earth –

NURI: I'm not going to help you.

LUCY: Talk to your dad. Please. I know he's the one in charge. He comes to the fence and deliberately throws rubbish into my dad's garden, deliberately all over his flower beds, the roses, breaking them, crushing them. Then laughs! He laughs at my dad and sticks his fingers up at him. He pisses over the fence into the garden!

NURI: Does your dad listen to you?

LUCY: Yes, of course he … yes! Doesn't yours?

Nuri smirks. She pulls lavender out of her bag.

NURI: I could make lavender posies to sell at the market. That's what you'd like us to be doing, isn't it? Wandering about in floaty dresses, selling posies and telling fortunes.

LUCY: I'd rather you didn't exist.

NURI: How do you know I don't have magical powers? You've wandered off the path into the woods, after a Gypsy girl. How do you know you're safe?

LUCY: Because if you lay one finger on me the police will come down on you so fast, you'll … actually, do it! Come on! Hurt me! Then the police will have to do something.

NURI: The police don't need an excuse.

LUCY: Do you even go to school? Can you even read the endless eviction letters you've been sent?

Nuri ignores her. She begins to form the lavender into bundles.

LUCY: Last week I tried walking to the shop. Just walking to the shop in my own neighborhood. And about five or six of your brothers or whatever, they followed me all the way, yelling at me, saying the most disgusting things. Yelling about what they wanted to do to me. How are they allowed?

NURI: They do that to me too.

LUCY: Why are they so disgusting?

NURI: Girls are not born good. They can sense it.

Pause.

NURI: My dad will move on when he wants to.

LUCY: You go back there now and tell him! You have to try!

NURI: I'm not going back there. So I can't tell him anything.

LUCY: You tell him or I swear to God I won't be held responsible for what I do –

NURI: I'm not going back!

LUCY: What do you mean you're not going back?

NURI: I can't now, can I. I'm covered in blood –

LUCY: It's only paint –

NURI: My reminder.

LUCY: Look, you got caught in the crossfire.

NURI: I was trying to get into the clinic. I couldn't though. All you lot, fucking yelling, with your banners. Then you started grabbing me, yelling in my face, then chasing me here!

LUCY: You're –

NURI: Yes. I am.

Pause.

LUCY: Ok. So what's the problem? You lot are all … you're all young. You have child brides! I read about it, it's disgusting!

NURI: It's disgusting to get pregnant but it's wrong to get rid of it?

LUCY: They just marry you off!

NURI: I'm not married, never can now. So what do you suggest I do, curse it away? What would your dad do if you got pregnant?

LUCY: He wouldn't let me murder it for starters! Destroy an unborn, helpless foetus! It would never happen anyway, I'm not stupid.

NURI: You haven't answered my question.

LUCY: He'd support me. He'd love me anyway.

NURI: My dad will kick me out. The whole community will turn against me. Today was … that's it. I can't go back to the clinic now. Someone will have spotted me, the way you were yelling fucking Gyppo at the top of your lungs. Someone will have seen. I can't get rid of it and I can't go home. So leave me alone now, will you?

Pause.

LUCY: What are are you going to do?

NURI: I don't know.

LUCY: Look, I didn't realise –

NURI: What if you had? Listen everyone! This one here, she's legit. She doesn't have a choice. Let her go in and have the fucking abortion cos otherwise she's going to get kicked out, she'll be on the street. She'll never see her family again.

LUCY: It's wrong to kill –

NURI: Shut up and go home to daddy.

Pause.

LUCY: You need to go into town, declare yourself homeless. If they know you're pregnant they might give you priority, maybe a flat or something.

NURI: What state scroungers we are! And never paid our taxes! What makes us think we deserve anything –

LUCY: Look –

NURI: You said it.

Pause.

NURI: I want my mum.
LUCY: Where is she?

Pause.
Lucy picks up the lavender and sniffs it.

LUCY: I used to come down here with my sister. We used to pretend we were
    orphans and there were witches chasing us. Then we'd get a thrashing for
    being all dirty.
NURI: Then what?
LUCY: What?
NURI: Then what happened?
LUCY: What are you talking about?
NURI: Get all tucked up with cocoa, did you?
LUCY: Who's the father?
NURI: Fuck off.
LUCY: Oh God.
NURI: What?
LUCY: That's why you can't talk to him!
NURI: What are you –
LUCY: Oh God. You need to go to the police. You need to tell someone.
NURI: Tell what?
LUCY: What do you think? That you've been knocked up by your dad –

In one swift action Nuri pulls the knife back out and throws herself onto Lucy,
pinning her against a tree.

NURI: You jumped up posh little bitch. How dare you!
LUCY: Get off me!
NURI: It wasn't my dad, you prissy little cunt!
LUCY: Ok I'm sorry! Back off will you? I made an assumption. I'm sorry.
NURI: I'm a little bit sick to fucking death of your assumptions. You're a snob!
    You're wicked, the way you were yelling at those women today, at us,
    passing judgement. And you complain when our boys yell at you! What's
    the difference?
LUCY: That is not the same thing –
NURI: A few weeks ago I was walking in the street. And some of your lot
    chased me! Shouting things out, horrible things, but nobody bats an eyelid
    at that. People want it, they think – the more aggro we get, the more likely
    it is that we'll just move on! They chased me all the way back to the field,
    all the way to the boundary fence. And you know why I ran for the fence?
    Do you?
LUCY: No.
NURI: Because your dad was in the garden, pruning his fucking roses. So I ran
    to the fence, the one my dad has pissed over so many times. I ran to the dip,

where the wood is rotten, and I yelled. I yelled at him, I yelled and yelled at your dad to help me. To please, for the love of God, help me. And then they caught up with me. There were three of them. And your dad? He watched. He stood, holding some dead roses in one hand, a spade in the other, and he watched. Until it was all over. He watched.

Silence.

LUCY: Why would you say that?
NURI: And so here we are.
LUCY: Why would you say that?
NURI: Little lost orphans in the wood. Because can you go home now?
LUCY: Please. I'm begging you –
NURI: Make it not true?

Pause.

LUCY: Tell me he didn't.
NURI: I can't. I'm sorry. I wish it weren't … I wish so much for such a lot of things not to be true.
LUCY: I don't believe you.
NURI: Do you not? I can't help that. Now let's just sit for a while, can we? Can we just do that? I'm tired. I just want to sit where it's peaceful for a bit.

She reaches for some lavender.

NURI: Take some. You just pull off some twine and wrap it round, tightly. Don't make a knot, just wrap till it's secure.

She hands Lucy some lavender and sits. Lucy remains standing.

NURI: You can buy me a new T shirt by the way. This smell reminds me of my mum. Makes me calm.
LUCY: I need to ask him myself.
NURI: Don't cross bridges, she used to say. She was the Phuri Da. You know what that is?
LUCY: No.
NURI: It meant she took care of the women and girls in the group. All of them, not just her own. She cared for all of them. I guess she meant don't go any-where you can't get back from. Can't get home.
LUCY: Why do you have lavender?
NURI: I was going to make a grave. Somewhere to come. I was going to leave lavender for her.
LUCY: Her?
NURI: Yes.

LUCY: What's going to happen?
NURI: We'll think of something.
LUCY: You and the baby?
NURI: And you? What are you going to do?

Lucy doesn't answer. Eventually she sits down beside Nuri and picks up some lavender.
Slowly the lights fade.

Ends.

Afterword

Katherine Manners

The title of this short play is a quote from *My Mother Said I Never Should* by Charlotte Keatley. I wanted to set the play by the railway line in Charlotte's play, where her characters meet as children in a world where different rules apply. Nuri represents another world, one that has clashed brutally with Lucy's. I wanted the play to cover an immense distance in a short space of time – at the start the girls are on opposing sides, sworn enemies, but by the end neither is able to go home, their bridges have been burned, and they must choose to trust each other and unite in order to survive.

Part II

'Love is like quicksilver in the hand. Leave the fingers open and it stays. Clutch it, and it darts away' (Dorothy Parker)

5   *Consolea*

Laura Jayne Ayres

Characters

FREDI, *female, 25, any accent, any ethnicity.*
OLIVER, *male, in his twenties, any accent, any ethnicity. He wears a shirt with a cactus pattern.*
WAITER, *any gender, age, accent, ethnicity.*

Notes

(–) at the end of a line indicates being cut off.
(…) indicates where speech trails off.

Original production details

Consolea was commissioned and produced by Little Pieces of Gold at South-wark Playhouse on 4 February 2018.

The cast was as follows:

FREDI	Laura Evelyn
OLIVER	Solomon Mousley
WAITRESS	Katherine Bennett Fox
Director:	Lydia Parker

Oliver and Fredi sit on perpendicular sides of a square table, as if squashed into a corner of a bistro. There is a red-checked tablecloth and a little vase of bright, but non-intrusive flowers. They are finishing a meal – a main course, at least. This is their second date, and it's going well. They talk quickly over one another, and are full of encouragement and joy. It's a cheering scene, and we are joining them very much mid-flow.

OLIVER: Oh, thanks! It's my cool shirt.
FREDI: Cacti is a very on-trend motif right now.

OLIVER: Well I am a very trendy, on-trend guy.

FREDI: 'Trendy' is such a mum word.

OLIVER: True. People who say 'trendy' aren't trendy.

FREDI: 'Trendy' – it actually sounds like a Mum name. Like Wendy.

OLIVER: Trendy. Trennndy.

FREDI: 'And this is my mum, Trendy.'

OLIVER: Trendy. It's lost all meaning.

FREDI: Well, I like your trendy shirt. Love a nice cactus.

OLIVER: The source of tequila.

FREDI: Exactly. And very low maintenance. I am enjoying the racing stripe.

OLIVER: The what now?

FREDI: That big great stripe? Across the sleeve?

Oliver looks at this shirt sleeve and is surprised to find a great big, grey mark across it, which is obviously not supposed to be there.

OLIVER: Oh no! (He tries to wipe it off, to no avail) My cool shirt!

FREDI: Did you not know? … How?

OLIVER: It must have been … I got trapped in the train doors on the way here.

FREDI: Oh no … one of those guys! And I was just starting to like you.

OLIVER: What guys?

FREDI The ones who jump in when the doors are closing and hold eeeeeverybody up because they Must Get On This Train –

OLIVER: It's not like that! Although – that is what happened.

FREDI: You people have a problem.

OLIVER: Not my people! I had a reason!

FREDI: Go on.

OLIVER: Well … it's – a bit of a silly reason.

FREDI: (With amused suspicion) Go on …

OLIVER: Well I had a choice of trains, and…. One would have made me – fashionably late, and the other one would make me eight minutes early and – and….

FREDI: And?

OLIVER: Well I didn't want to be too keen and early –

FREDI: And we know you are very fashionable –

OLIVER: Right?! But then – I panicked, you know? I didn't want you to think I'd stood you up – and I had made it in time for the first train anyway, so –

FREDI: (With a laugh – she is finding this endearing) So?

OLIVER: I just – I heard the beeping of the doors and suddenly I knew … I just knew I couldn't pull off fashionably late and my legs just took over and – yeah, I leapt onto the train. Quite a majestic leap.

FREDI: Like a salmon.

OLIVER: A bit like a salmon, yeah – in a cool shirt – trapped in the closing doors.

FREDI: Did people glare at you? When the train moved off?

OLIVER: People glared.

FREDI: I would have glared. I always glare.

OLIVER: There was a bit of tutting. And now I have the Stripe of Shame.

FREDI: Punishment enough! This place is nice – very French.

OLIVER: The spag bol is probably technically not that French but this one is just so good.

FREDI: Are you an aficionado?

OLIVER: Yes. A sommelier of spag bol. No, a connoisseur.

FREDI: A seasoned spag-bolista.

OLIVER: Pun!

FREDI: Sort of a pun?

OLIVER: I always want to try something new but … the spag bol, it calls to me.

FREDI: (In a Gollum voice) My precious.

OLIVER: What?

FREDI: (She realises explaining herself will just look weird, and brushes it off with a laugh) Never mind. Oooo – I'm stuffed.

OLIVER: Me too. That was great.

FREDI: So great? It's still light outside, I think. Do you…. We could go for a walk?

OLIVER: Walk it off. Yeah – that would be nice. A digestif.

FREDI: Très French.

There is a little pause. Something is stopping Oliver. Does Fredi sense it?

FREDI: Shall we….

OLIVER: Can I ask you something?

FREDI: Mais oui.

OLIVER: I don't know if it's allowed.

FREDI: Go for it.

OLIVER: Okay, well…. You're wearing a wedding ring. And an engagement ring.

FREDI: (With a little laugh, but with the weight of having been asked this before) That's not technically a question.

OLIVER: True. It's not.

FREDI: But fair enough. It's a fair not-question. I'm not married. Or engaged.

OLIVER: I see. Right. Well. I don't see. But I don't mind if….

FREDI: If?

OLIVER: If there's something you don't want to explain. Or if there's nothing to explain.

FREDI: No, no it's okay. There is a reason. I'm not married though. I am not currently married. I am not now, but … – yeah I have been married.

OLIVER: Oh … right. So –

FREDI: I used to have a husband. He gave me the rings, and … I haven't taken them off yet.

OLIVER: (Trying to understand) Fair enough. That seems…. Up to you.

FREDI: It's not like, a divorce, or anything.

OLIVER: (Still confused) Oh. Right.

FREDI: He's dead. He died.

OLIVER: Oh.

FREDI: So. Yeah. I'm a widow.

OLIVER: Oh. Fuck.

FREDI: Yeah. Fuck. He was really nice. He was cool. You're not in trouble for asking.

OLIVER: I'm so sorry.

FREDI: It's okay. I mean it was a very valid and definitely relevant question.

OLIVER: No I mean, I'm sorry – I'm sorry that that happened to you.

FREDI Oh. Thank you. Thanks.

OLIVER: Wow.

FREDI: Yeah.

OLIVER: When – when did....

FREDI: When did I become a widow?

OLIVER: Sorry.

FREDI: (Kindly) Don't be.

OLIVER: Sorry.

FREDI: In 2014. I was 22. I just turned 22.

OLIVER: Christ.

FREDI: I'm 25 now.

OLIVER: Yeah.

FREDI: (Tapping her head, trying to make a joke) Maths. Don't worry … it still sounds baffling to me, too. It's not to be expected.

OLIVER: I'm – sorry that bafflement is what's mainly coming across.

FREDI: Don't be! It's absolutely fair.

OLIVER: You're very – you're so young.

FREDI: I am. Widow is a very olden-days word.

OLIVER: Yes – yes it really is. You don't look like –

FREDI: Like what? Like a crinkly old lady?

OLIVER: No! I mean – no. God, no – you don't but –

FREDI: I'm being silly! I'm just being silly.

Oliver is struggling. Widows generally don't look 25. Widows generally are not 25.

OLIVER: No. I think that's what I meant?

FREDI: We got married quite young and he – he died very young. So....

Oliver is blank.

FREDI: … We knew. That it was going to happen.

OLIVER: Christ. That's … I'm sorry.

FREDI: Me too. He was very cool. And they're nice rings, so – You're actually dealing with this quite well.

OLIVER: Really?!

FREDI: Oh yes. There have been some quite spectacular reactions.

OLIVER: Like what?

FREDI: Well nobody is ever expecting it, of course – because why would you? – (With warmth) '25-year-old-widow' is not a very catchy or … entrancing Tinder bio, is it?

OLIVER: (Relaxing a little) Well, no.

FREDI: So it really catches people off guard. But you're being very chill.

OLIVER: Thank you. Likewise? But I'm not the one who should be … who –

FREDI: I am quite practised now, in fairness. One guy just got up and left. When I told him.

OLIVER: No! Just like that?

FREDI: Yep! Opened and closed his mouth a few times, goldfish style.… And then yep. Folded his napkin, weirdly neatly and then, yeah – tucked his chair in and left.

OLIVER: Without paying?! Oh god, sorry – sorry that's so not the point at all.

FREDI: No absolutely! That was my first thought anyway.… But actually I had a voucher – from a friend of a friend, so it was going to be on me anyway, but –

OLIVER: But still –

FREDI: Yep. Off he went. We just ordered pudding though so I got to eat his. Silver linings –

OLIVER: Silver linings –

FREDI: Exactly! So it was quite fun in the end?

OLIVER: Probably better off?

FREDI: Oh, for sure. And there was another guy who just burst into tears – I mean we were quite drunk by this point and I think he was just blindsided and yeah –

OLIVER: No –

FREDI: He kept calling it a tragedy? I'm not very good at crying people –

OLIVER: Me neither.

FREDI: Yeah – anyone – Girls, boys … my dog when I leave the house.…

OLIVER: Oh that's a very sad sound isn't it. A real lament!

FREDI: Very lamentatious. Lamenting? She's a Labrador.

OLIVER: The friendliest dogs!

FREDI: (Agreement) The silliest.

OLIVER: She sounds fun.

FREDI: Because she's a Labrador?

OLIVER: Well, mainly, yeah. I like dogs.

FREDI: You'd like her then. Sally.

OLIVER: We should hang out some time.

FREDI: She would like that. I would, also.

OLIVER: (Realising he has accidentally asked her out again) Cool. Cool.

FREDI: You are being cool about this. In your cool shirt.

OLIVER: I'm sorry that guy ran out on you.

FREDI: Oh, I'm not – it's fine.

OLIVER: And that I went a bit quiet. I'm not good at knowing what to say in … situations.

FREDI: I don't think anybody is, though. I mean – if you had told me you were a widow – a widower – I probably would have still done the same as you, just – said sorry a lot? (Inhale. This is rehearsed –) I know you might go home and think about this a lot and decide it's baggage and – that's okay –

OLIVER: I wasn't … I mean – it's not the plan –

FREDI: But I can understand. You are also 25? So – it's understandable.

OLIVER: It's not the plan … I – I like you.

FREDI: Good. Cool. Well, I like you. I'm very glad you're not another runner. For a moment I thought you might leg it –

OLIVER: Oh no!

FREDI: But you didn't, and … That's cool. Thanks.

OLIVER: Cool.

FREDI: Cool.

(Smiles a bright, clearing smile.)

I just have to go to the loo, before we go – Shall we get the bill?

OLIVER: Yes. Yeah let's get the bill. I'll get it.

FREDI: Be right back.

She gets up, picks her napkin up and jokily folds it – weirdly neatly – on the table then heads off to the loo.

Oliver watches her go. He signals over to a waiter and asks for the bill using the international 'can we get the bill' pretend hand signature. Deep exhale. He slowly, somewhat absent-mindedly, folds his napkin into a swan, and leaves it on the table. After a pause, he suddenly downs his drink, taps the table, and heads towards the door, quickly. Exits.

After a second, Fredi returns. She is smiling, like she has just seen something funny she wants to share, and then sees the empty table. She goes over to it, looking at Oliver's seat, briefly looking around for him. She notices the swan napkin. She picks it up, it unravels in her hand. She stares at it, and sits down. As she sits, a waiter brings the bill.

WAITER: Aaaaaand here's your bill – is there anything else I can get for you?

FREDI: No – no thanks. Did you see him leave?

WAITER: Sorry?

FREDI: The guy sitting here? Is he – did he leave?

WAITER: He asked for the bill, but – actually I did see him heading out of the door, yeah.

FREDI: Oh.

WAITER: I assumed he's left cash, and – yeah. He looked like he was in a rush. Sorry.

FREDI: A rush to leave. Cool. I'll – I guess I'm paying by card.

WAITER: I'll just go and grab the machine.

FREDI: Thanks.

Fredi lets out a deep sigh. She wasn't expecting this, and it's a disappointment. She fiddles with the napkin. Gets her purse out, as the waiter comes back over.

WAITER: If you just pop your card in there and check the amount?

She does so. Puts her PIN in, receipts are transferred, etc.

WAITER: That's great! Thanks very much for coming, hope you enjoyed your, er … date.
FREDI: Thanks. The food was great.
WAITER: (Leaving, awkward) Thanks!

Fredi sits a little blankly, the napkin in her lap. She picks it up, looks at it and lets out a long breath. Is she giving him a chance to return? She decides he isn't going to. Puts the napkin on the table in a crumpled heap, quite forcefully. Picks up her bag, puts jacket on. Shakes her head, perhaps a little laugh of disbelief. She is just tucking her chair in, when –

Oliver has stumbled back in. He is breathing very heavily. He is carrying a little potted cactus. He smiles with relief.

OLIVER: Oh thank god! Thank god you're still here.
FREDI: I was just leaving.
OLIVER: I'm so sorry! I'm so – (he is very out of breath)
FREDI: Wh?
OLIVER: (Gasping) Flowers – I saw – flowers. A florist. On the corner.
FREDI: Now?
OLIVER: No – before…. Before – god I am so unfit.
FREDI: (Unsure) You are.
OLIVER: There is a florist on the corner – and – I didn't know whether to get you flowers – before this, before the date –
FREDI: And you decided not to….
OLIVER: Well, yeah – yeah – I dunno. It didn't feel – yeah I dunno. But I'm glad I didn't.
FREDI: Okay….?
OLIVER: But I wanted to get you something. Now – after – this evening, this conversation. I wanted to have got them for you. But flowers was wrong, so –
FREDI: So you've brought me a little cactus.
OLIVER: Yes – I've – brought you a little cactus.
FREDI: To match your shirt.
OLIVER: Sort of to match my shirt but it seemed like the right – idea. It's – I dunno.
FREDI: Because I am prickly?
OLIVER: No! Because – no – because. You are still here.
FREDI: Well I wasn't going to do a runner on myself.
OLIVER: No – oh god – neither was I! That was bad timing. The card machine – I wanted to come back before you got back and it would be a – surprise.

FREDI: I was quite surprised that you were not here.

OLIVER: Sorry – yeah, god that must have looked bad.

FREDI: It did look bad.

OLIVER: Really bad – quite bad planning, from me.

Fredi laughs. This is endearing, luckily. Oliver is still clutching onto the cactus.

OLIVER: But this is for you. Because – You are here, being – verdant, and – resilient, and –

FREDI: (Nodding, gentle mock-wisdom) It's a metaphor.

OLIVER: It is, it is – verdant is maybe not right – I just … I thought it was going to be really cute but I'm quite unfit and there was a minimum card charge, and –

FREDI: I like it.

OLIVER: You do?

FREDI: I do. It's very cute. It's a cute cactus. That was cute, of you. Badly timed, but, yeah – cute.

OLIVER: Thank you. And sorry. And – thanks.

Oh, you paid!

FREDI: I did pay. Just. I've just paid.

OLIVER: God – dreadful timing.

FREDI: Dreadful timing. Now you owe me dinner.

OLIVER: I do owe you dinner. I would really like to buy another dinner for you.

FREDI: Now? I'm quite full –

OLIVER: No, no, not now, another –

FREDI: I'm joking! I'm joking. I know.

OLIVER: Another time. A further time.

FREDI: I would like that. I would really like that.

He presents the cactus to her – she happily accepts.

FREDI: Thank you.

OLIVER: Thank you. For – this was good.

FREDI: This was good. Would you still like to go for a walk?

Oliver smiles, nods – yes, he would. They grin.

Ends.

Afterword

Laura Jayne Ayres

I began writing *Consolea* right in the middle of the drama – the moment where Fredi reveals she is a widow. I knew I wanted to write about how a young woman might deal with widowhood in a world where Tinder dates are more common than young married couples. I was fascinated by the idea that someone my age might be going on a date having already lived through a whole marriage in their early twenties; it's something that might be surprising to hear about now, but a hundred years ago might not have seemed so unusual. The first few dates of any relationship can be filled with awkward moments and I wanted to try and create something that was still reassuring and warm, despite the curveballs. It was very important to me that Fredi wasn't presented as a tragic figure; whatever might have happened to her, she is unapologetically witty, silly and romantic.

6   *Alive Day*

Fran Bushe

Characters

ARLA, *early thirties, female.*
SIMON, *early thirties, male.*

Notes

(–) at the end of a line indicates being cut off.
(…) indicates where speech trails off.
(/) indicates the point where the immediately following dialogue interrupts.
(Beat) indicates a brief break in the dialogue.
(Pause) indicates where there is a thought process happening.

Original production details

Alive Day was commissioned and produced by Little Pieces of Gold at South-wark Playhouse on 23 April 2017.

The cast was as follows:

ARLA	Leah Lawry-Johns
SIMON	Matt Harrison-James
Director:	Hannah Jones

Arla and Simon's living room. Simon enters. He puts down his bag and shim-mies awkwardly and uncomfortably out of his coat. Arla springs out from behind a chair where she's been hiding, popping a party popper as she does so. She is wearing a novelty hooded onesie and an apron. Her hair is unbrushed and she looks wild. Arla runs and jumps into Simon's arms.

ARLA: ALIIIIIIIIIIIIIIIIIIIIIVE!
SIMON: Shit it's –
ARLA: ALIIIIIVE! Alive! Alive! Alive-alive-alive. A-LIVE. A-live.

Arla begins to dance and twerk around Simon.

SIMON: It's your birthday, shit I'm, is it your/

ARLA: No! No. Aliiive! Aliiiiiiive. Hakuna Matata!

SIMON: Anniversary? It's not our anniversary, our anniversary is in/June.

ARLA: June. This isn't an anniversary. Alive. Alive! Al –

SIMON: Anniversary of something else? First date? First kiss? First shag? They were all the same day though I guess so … all of those?

ARLA: Simon please, listen. It's Alive Day! ALIVE DAY!

SIMON: I still don't understand what that means.

ARLA: ALIIIIIVE!

SIMON: It's your mum's birthday?

ARLA: Happy Alive Day! ALIVE DAY!

SIMON: Is that a real day? Should I have got you a card?

ARLA: It's today. And also the next day. And the next. And for however long you have/left –

SIMON: Don't.

ARLA: What?

SIMON: Don't.

ARLA: Don't?

SIMON: Say it.

ARLA: What? Say what?

SIMON: That. It. Don't say … that.

ARLA: Oh … Ok. I know. I got this. I've got the hang of not saying it. I'm getting better at not saying it. I was going to end the sentence there.

SIMON: Also don't say passed over or gone

ARLA: I won't.

SIMON: Or gone over to the other side.

ARLA: I'm not a medium, why would I say – ?

SIMON: Don't say it.

ARLA: I won't say it, I'm not going to say it.

SIMON: Let's change the –

ARLA: For however long we have, Comma, we are going to celebrate being alive. ALIIIIIIIIVE.

She begins to dance again around the room.

SIMON: Arla –

ARLA: We are going to make every single one of your heart beats count.

SIMON: I need to go take a shower.

ARLA: I've made all of your favourite foods. All of them. You will never for as long as you live have to eat a mouthful that you think is mediocre or average. Apathy is no longer an emotion you are going to experience. Goodbye apathy, hello aliiiive.

SIMON: Please stop this, this is making me –

ARLA: And I've booked your favourite band for this evening and you are going to sing with them and record an original track with them!

SIMON: What? Shit, that's –

ARLA: I know! Alive!

SIMON: You've booked Oasis?

ARLA: Why Oa...

SIMON: Well they are my favourite band.

ARLA: I thought ... Ok no, it's fine, it's fine. I can change that, that's not a –

SIMON: Since I was a kid.

ARLA: I just thought that –

SIMON: It's pretty obvious –

ARLA: I really didn't think Oasis were your favourite –

SIMON: I mean I sleep in a Morning Glory t-shirt.

ARLA: Pyjamas, right. Yeah I didn't think that's what that was referring to.

SIMON: Well it's –

ARLA: Always thought that was a reference to –

SIMON: And the posters and y'know gigs but it's –

ARLA: Sure, right, well that makes (Beat). Yep. Well I'll, I can change that, I can. Shit, do not worry. Don't be disappointed. Disappointment is also a feeling you will no longer experience! Goodbye disappointment. It's banned.

SIMON: They have always been my favourite band. Forever

ARLA: I've just never ... Never mind.

Pause.

I've got some drugs.

SIMON: Drugs?

ARLA: I've got so many drugs.

SIMON: We don't do drugs. We've never done drugs. We're not the types to do drugs.

ARLA: I know! Aliiiiive! I'm also first aid trained.

SIMON: Why is that important?

ARLA: Because drugs kill. They can kill ... I'm trained if anything goes ... wrong.

SIMON: I have no interest in –

ARLA: We could start with some coke.

SIMON: Arla. Look at me. I don't want to take drugs. If they mix with my pills then it could be really –

ARLA: Hey, we don't worry about things like that on Alive Day.

She pulls out a small bag of white powder and starts pouring enthusiastically onto a surface. Sits and quietly stares at it.

ARLA: So you just...

SIMON: Having trouble?

ARLA: Just trying to work out … how to … how to.…

SIMON: Let's not do drugs.

ARLA I: I've seen it in films … but when you're faced with all this white –

SIMON: You don't need to –

ARLA: I'll You Tube it, they'll have a tutorial.

SIMON: Please put the coke away Arla.

ARLA: In films they always chop it up with a little card, don't they, pass me your wallet, should I. … chop it up? Chop it up right?

SIMON: I have a Boots advantage card?

ARLA: That's not sexy, not rock and roll sexy enough. Give it.

He passes it to her. She pushes the powder around with the card, no idea at all what she is doing.

ARLA: Shit, I don't know what I'm doing, I don't know how to –

SIMON: We don't need to –

Arla plants one side of her face directly into the coke. It stings her eyes and none goes up her nose. Simon pulls her out of her coke pile and begins to de-coke her face.

ARLA: I'm not great putting things up my nose.

SIMON: So don't.

ARLA: Can't even put that Vicks stuff up –

SIMON: It's all over your –

ARLA: The nose stuff, for blocked noses, menthol nose stuff, y'know?

SIMON: Please stop this.

She takes another dive at the coke but Simon has her in his arms.

ARLA: It's fine, we don't have to do coke, coke is a bit of a shit drug anyway. It's probably just talcum powder and chalk and … I've got others … I got some ice.

SIMON: I don't know what ice is.

ARLA: Crystal meth.

SIMON: Arla!

ARLA: I got us crystal meth, and also pills and weed, lots of weed if you weren't feeling, weren't feeling like giving crystal meth a go, although it was quite expensive, so it'd be a bit wasteful, but I get it. Because it's quite a –

SIMON: Yeah, it is, it's quite a, I mean I think it's how people become homeless right?

ARLA: Quite a big … drug yeah. Teeth fall out and y'know –

SIMON: And I like my teeth.

ARLA: I like your teeth too.

Pause.

ARLA: But maybe we should be homeless! ... Shouldn't we experience proper poverty before (Beat). Sorry, I didn't say it. I didn't. But maybe ... Boxes, alleyways, sleeping under the stars. That's pretty alive! We're so ... privileged! Let's fuck our privilege!

SIMON: Fuck our ... fuck our privilege?

ARLA: We said we'd do all the drugs when we hit 90 but that plan's out the window because ... Well because nothing. So here we go. And I've got all the films that are in the 100 top films to watch before you. (Beat) Shit. Sorry. I didn't say anything. I didn't say that. I didn't.

SIMON: This isn't what I want.

ARLA: And anytime you want to have sex.

SIMON: Oh?

ARLA: Just say.

SIMON: That's really ... generous but –

ARLA: Just let me know, within reason and we can. And if y'know there's anything that you want to try. Within reason. I'm happy to, probably, give it a go, probably.

SIMON: That's. Nice of you.

She hurriedly and messily takes off her apron.

ARLA: I'm not wearing any pants, just so I can be ... ready ... I'm prepared. Do you want to now?

She begins to undo the top buttons on her onesie, but he does them back up as fast as she undoes them.

SIMON: I'm alright thanks.

ARLA: Ok. Ok. It doesn't have to be ... now.

SIMON: It's a lovely offer, a really great nice offer but –

ARLA: A threesome? Foursome?

SIMON: Wo –

ARLA: Or someone else? I could watch. Or not watch. Or film it and –

SIMON: You need to stop this.

ARLA: Or if you wanted to try with a man. I honestly wouldn't mind. It's about you. I want you to embrace life. This life. And whatever that might involve is fine. Live in the now! This is me giving my consent and we are just animals right? Right! If we were monkeys we'd be just fucking each other left right and centre, right, non-stop fuck fuck fuckity fuck fuck.

SIMON: Arla –

Arla's composure begins to break.

ARLA: Fuck fuck fuck. Fuck. Fuck. Fuck. Fuck.

SIMON: You're being –

ARLA: And if you were worried that you haven't slept with enough people, we can sort that out too, I made a list … of women … who I wouldn't mind, in the circumstances and they wouldn't mind.

SIMON: Calm down.

ARLA: And we can contact them.

SIMON: I don't want anyone else.

ARLA: Together. We could interview them.

SIMON: You are being mad. This now, this now, feels mad.

ARLA: Is mad good? Mad is alive right? Living on the edge? Who wants to live sane? Not me. Aliiiiiiive.

SIMON: I know this is hard.

ARLA: We can live so much, do so much in the time you have (Beat) doing the things you really want to do. Some people. Most people. They won't have done, achieved anything in the time you have (Beat). They'll just sit at desks and spin on spinny chairs and eat … stuffed crusts.

SIMON: I like stuffed crusts.

ARLA: I know, I've hand made you some. It said in all the pamphlets and books that homemade things, show the person who is (Beat) that you really. Care. I really. Care.

SIMON: Ok, stop this now, I need to/

ARLA: I made you Bakewell tarts and homemade French fancies, like Mr Kipling, although not quite as fancy, his are … fancier.

SIMON: I just need a moment, I –

ARLA: I worked so hard.

SIMON: I just want calm and to sit and maybe drink a tea. I'm going to take a shower.

ARLA: No.

SIMON: Clear my –

ARLA: Don't.

SIMON: I won't be a moment.

ARLA: Can I come?

SIMON: For a shower?

ARLA: Yes. Or don't go. Or I can just sit outside the door?

SIMON: Arla –

ARLA: Don't do any living without me there, I don't want to waste a minute. Please stay. Stay.

Please. Stay with me, don't go.

SIMON: Ok I'll stay. I won't take a shower.

Pause.

ARLA: I mean. Don't go. Ever.

Pause.
They hold each other.

ARLA: Please don't. Y'know –
SIMON: Ok/
ARLA: Ok.
SIMON: Yeah I won't, as simple as that.

Pause.

ARLA: How are you feeling?
SIMON: Right now I'm pretending it's happening to someone else.
ARLA: Who?
SIMON: Jack Black.
ARLA: My ex Jack Black, or the famous Jack Black?
SIMON: Guess.

She holds his face in her hands.

ARLA: Simon.
SIMON: Make it go away.
ARLA: I can't.
SIMON: Make it go backwards.
ARLA: I –
SIMON: Make it stop.
ARLA: I wish I –
SIMON: Make it.
ARLA: I –
SIMON: Make it not me.
ARLA: I would.
SIMON: Anyone else.
ARLA: Anyone else.
SIMON: Don't go.
ARLA: I'm not.
SIMON: Hold. Hold me.
ARLA: I am.
SIMON: Don't think about it.
ARLA: I'm –
SIMON: Stop thinking about –
ARLA: I'm not.
SIMON: Are. Can tell. Can feel you are. Stop.
ARLA: Don't know how.
SIMON: Think about something else.
ARLA: What else?
SIMON: I don't know if I'm doing this right.
ARLA: It's just a hug, you're doing it great.
SIMON: Ha –
ARLA: There isn't a. A right way.

SIMON: I could have done things better.

ARLA: You did things great.

SIMON: Did?

ARLA: Did.

SIMON: No past tense.

ARLA: Sorry I –

SIMON: Am doing, am doing, am doing, I am current, I am here, I am present. I'm here.

ARLA: You are here. We could just stand like this.

SIMON: Until –

ARLA: Until. Just us.

SIMON: This isn't easy … on you. For you.

ARLA: It's ok.

SIMON: If it's any consolation, it's shit for me, really shit. Everything just became so much more. Urgent. Important. Precious. But also worthless and pointless.

ARLA: I just wanted to make it good. Make everything good. For you. Give you something. To live for. Give me something. To live for.

Pause.

SIMON: What will it be like once I've. Once I. What will you do first?

ARLA: What?

SIMON: When I'm …

ARLA: I don't want to think about it.

SIMON: What will be your first meal?

ARLA: Simon –

SIMON: Where will you do your first shop?

ARLA: Shhh.

SIMON: When will you next say I love you to someone?

ARLA: Please stop. Stop it.

SIMON: Will you open a new box of condoms or just keep going from the same one we're using?

ARLA: Simon, stop it, that's not –

SIMON: I mean it's a value pack, so it's quite a lot of condoms, be silly to buy a whole new –

ARLA: It's not fair, stop it, stop it, stop it.

Pause. A long one. They are far apart in all the ways.

ARLA: Noodles.

SIMON: What?

ARLA: Noodles.

SIMON: Noodles?

ARLA: Noodles. Tesco.

SIMON: Oh no shh, I was –

ARLA: My first meal. I won't feel like cooking so I'll order take away and I won't be able to make any decisions so I'll choose the thing at the top of the menu. Noodles. I won't feel like walking very far so I'll go to Tesco and it'll be for milk because I won't know what else to do. Other than make tea. And I can't imagine. I can't imagine. Someone else. Loving someone else. (Beat) And it'll be so far in the future, we'll probably have invented an alternative to condoms by then ... some sort of electro ... sperm ... magnet.

SIMON: A coil!?

ARLA: That's not how a coil works.

SIMON: It isn't happening. Is it?

ARLA: It isn't happening.

SIMON: You believe that?

ARLA: I believe that.

SIMON: So we just keep living. We just keep going?

ARLA: We just keep going. Happy Alive day.

SIMON: Aliiiiiiive.

The sound of a baby crying from upstairs.

SIMON: What's that?

ARLA: I –

SIMON: What is –

ARLA: Uhh Simon.

SIMON: Is that –

ARLA: Nothing, it's really, nothing –

SIMON: A baby? It's –

ARLA: Not a baby, not, no.

SIMON: A crying baby, Arla.

ARLA: No. Not a crying baby, not –

SIMON: Arla ... what have you done?

ARLA: Simon I –

SIMON: Where did you get a baby?

ARLA: I wanted you to have everything ... I wanted you to experience every-thing.... Everything. Before you, before you –

Ends.

Afterword

Fran Bushe

Alive Day tells the story of a couple dealing with a bereavement before it has happened. I wanted to write about how knowing you are going to lose someone changes the nature of time passing and the weight of the moments you have with that person. Each second becomes horribly precious and heavily important. This play explores how Arla and Simon navigate the unthinkable. They are each other's worlds.

I imagined a story where both members of a couple try alternately to shield and protect each other from harm, whilst simultaneously trying hopelessly to stay strong for the other. The play should feel like it could fall apart at any moment through the weight of what they are facing and pace can be played with to create the idea of losing time. I hope in these characters you will find a love story, courage and an intense drive to be alive. This piece is now being developed into a full-length play, *Watch List*.

7 *Love By Numbers*

Joanne Lau

Characters

NATALIE, *34, British-born Chinese, potty-mouthed but sweet.*
MAX, *24, Scottish, happy-go-lucky.*

Notes

(–) at the end of a line indicates being cut off.
(…) at the end of a speech means it trails off. On its own it indicates a pressure or expectation to speak.

Original production details

Love By Numbers was commissioned and produced by Little Pieces of Gold at The Canal Café Theatre, 5–7 March 2018.

The cast was as follows:

NATALIE	Rebecca Yeo
MAX	Tom Crowhurst
Director:	Jaclyn Bradley

Natalie sits alone in her lab coat. Before her on the table is a cage – a furry form just visible through the semi-transparent plastic and metal bars. She scribbles in her lab book.

NATALIE: Experiment 533955. Inoculation: 400 milligrams. Weight 1.2 kilos. Disease progression: 300 days. Termination: Day 301. (She directly addresses the audience) They're just numbers, really. Our lives, I mean. Age. Height. Weight. Stamps in your passport. Money in your bank account. Degrees. Wisdom teeth. The number of scars on your body. The number of people you've fucked. The number of times your heart has been broken … (To animal) 301. Today's day 301. I'm sorry 533955. I'm so, so sorry.

Tears fall silently as she picks up a syringe and fills it. At a noise, she hurriedly puts down the syringe and wipes the evidence of her emotions from her face.

Max bursts in dancing and singing badly to an unheard tune on his headphones.

NATALIE: (To audience) It's just Max. Number of weeks into this job? 8. Number of weeks I predict his youthful enthusiasm will last? 15. If he's lucky. (Smiles) Still, it's kind of sweet....

Max spots Natalie and immediately whips off his headphones.

MAX: Shit! Sorry! I didn't know anyone was still here!

NATALIE: Nice moves.

MAX: Aw, come on! Like you've never danced alone in the lab. I bet you do it all the time.

NATALIE: Nope! I don't know how to dance.

MAX: What?! Everyone knows how to dance!

NATALIE: (To audience) Number of times I've heard that in my life: 85.

MAX: Dancing's easy! You just feel the music!

NATALIE: Rocket science is easy. You just feel the physics.

MAX: Touché! So you always work this late?

NATALIE: No. Just lots to catch up today. (To audience) Number of lies I've just told: 1.

MAX: Well, do you want some help? I've just finished up.

NATALIE: Oh, no. You've probably got somewhere better to be.

MAX: (Too quickly) No I don't.

Beat.

NATALIE: (To audience) Number of lies he's just told: 1?

MAX: Really. All I've got to go home to is a furiously masturbating Scotsman and an oven pizza.

NATALIE: I thought you lived alone?

MAX: Aye. And I don't actually own an oven so I'd have to order the pizza in.

Natalie laughs. She pauses, thoughtful.

NATALIE: (To audience) That's the first time I've laughed in … I can't even remember.

MAX: So what is it you need to do with (reads cage label) 533955?

NATALIE: It's the end of the experiment. I have to cull him before the disease gets too far – before he starts to suffer. And I know I should, but I just … I can't bring myself to do it.

MAX: Can't you just do it next week? I mean, he looks fine. (To 533955) Don't you, you handsome devil?

NATALIE: He's not. It's hard to tell with rabbits sometimes. They're prey animals, so they tend to hide it when they're sick. You really have to know the animal and look carefully to spot anything's even wrong....

Max looks at her.

NATALIE: (To audience) Number of seconds he's been staring at me: 3 ... 4....

MAX: Why are you really here so late?

Natalie's mobile sounds in her pocket. She grabs it out.

NATALIE: It's Tom. I'd better just –

Max raises his eyebrows, but says nothing.

NATALIE: (Texting as she talks) He's hassling me about ordering food.

MAX: What's on the menu tonight?

NATALIE: Chinese.

MAX: Well. That makes sense.

NATALIE: Why's that?

MAX: Oh. Uh, I ...

NATALIE: (Smiles) I'm just fucking with you.

MAX: That is so mean! So, so mean!

NATALIE: Truth is, I don't even like Chinese takeaway. Tom loves it though.

MAX: What's wrong with Chinese takeaway?

NATALIE: Oh nothing! It's just – my parents had a Chinese takeaway, and to me, no one's food will ever be as good as my dad's.

MAX: Why don't you just order from your parents then? I bet you'd even get a discount – if you ordered over 10 pounds and picked it up in person.

NATALIE: Oh, uh, well, my dad passed, and my mum sold it after, so....

MAX: Shit. I'm so sorry. Stupid Max always running his stupid mouth. I'm sorry.

NATALIE: It's OK. I'm slowly getting used to the place Tom orders from. He always gets the same thing.

MAX: Oh yeah? What's that then?

NATALIE: Number 72: sweet and sour chicken balls. Number 83: special Yang Chow fried rice. And Number 25....

MAX: Number 25?

NATALIE: (To audience) The age I was when I started dating Tom. Number 30 – the age he was. Number 9 – the years we've been together. Number 3 – the times he's broken my heart. Number 4 – the times I've tried to leave him. 4 – the times I came back. I've tried ... I've tried ... I've tried....

MAX: Nat? Natalie?

NATALIE: Sorry. What were you saying?

MAX: Nothing. It wasn't important. Hey, I've never asked you – do you prefer

Nat or Natalie? 'Cause everyone around here calls you Nat, but you always sign your name Natalie in your emails.

NATALIE: I don't mind, really.

MAX: What you on about? It's your name!

NATALIE: Well, I guess I prefer Natalie, but everyone just naturally shortens it to Nat. Even Tom does it. "Tom and Nat!" No idea why. It's just one of those things, I guess.

MAX: Alright. Well, I'm going to start calling you Natalie – I mean, if that's what you prefer.

NATALIE: Thank you.

They smile at one another warmly. There's a definite moment.

NATALIE: (To audience) 177 centimetres. His height. Why am I suddenly thinking about that? My pulse is racing: 60 beats per minute. 63 … 68 … 72.…

Natalie grabs her phone to break to the tension.

NATALIE: It's getting late.

MAX: Then you'd better decide what to do with him.

NATALIE: (Staring at her phone) I guess deep down I know what I have to do, but it – It'd be so much easier if I just stayed with him – put up, shut up. I mean, we live together, we're engaged! I get on with his mum, and I – I'm not getting any younger. I want kids some day and –

MAX: I meant the rabbit.

NATALIE: Oh my gosh. Sorry. Oh my gosh.

MAX: No. Don't apologise.

NATALIE: I am so embarrassed right now. Shit. Shit!

MAX: That's why you're here late, isn't it? You don't want to go home.

NATALIE: Just pretend I didn't say anything! Forget everything you just heard!

She wipes furiously at her tears, angry for letting herself cry.

MAX: Hey. It'll be alright. The kids thing especially. I mean, you're what – 27?

Natalie laughs despite her tears.

MAX: 28? No. 30?

NATALIE: (Laughs harder) I'm 34. But thank you.

MAX: No way. You're 34?! No!

NATALIE: (Still laughing) Yay Asian genes! (Sees Max looking serious) What? What is it?

MAX: (Counting on his fingers) … plus seven … Oh good! It's fine.

NATALIE: What?

MAX: Nothing. So, uh Tom. You want to talk about it?

Natalie's smile drops.

NATALIE: Could I have one of your cigarettes?

MAX: How did you do that? How did you know I smoke? I haven't told anyone here!

NATALIE: You just have that sort of spontaneous recklessness about you. You need that to smoke. I mean, every breath is a willing act of self-destruction.

Max takes out his papers and tobacco and starts rolling her a cigarette.

MAX: Seriously? You think I'm reckless?

NATALIE: Nah. I just figured you for a smoker 'cause you're aging terribly.

MAX: (Laughs) That's probably true. People tell me I look 27 all the time.

NATALIE: Yeah. Same.

MAX: (Laughs) Fuck you.

He hands her the cigarette.

NATALIE: Thanks.

She twirls the cigarette in her fingers, thoughtful.

NATALIE: He doesn't love me. He doesn't love me and it – it hurts.

MAX: But he asked you to marry him?

NATALIE: Yeah.

MAX: But you don't have a ring?

NATALIE: Oh, it's – it was way too big for me and we just never got around to getting it adjusted.

MAX: How long ago was that?

NATALIE: Four years?

MAX: Uh huh.

NATALIE: I know! I know! It's just – Tom's just got this timeline, you know? Like go to uni, get a job, meet a girl, date for this many years, move in together after this long, get engaged ... but it's all on this set little schedule. He's got this arbitrary idea of what's "normal" and heaven forbid what his work friends might think if he doesn't do it all in the right order or at the right time.

MAX: That's –

NATALIE: No. Don't talk. If you say anything in his defence I will punch you in the fucking mouth. And if you agree with me and tell me how horrible he is, I'll just feel stupid and you'll seem all predatory.

MAX: Predatory?

NATALIE: Like one of those creepy shoulder-to-cry-on guys.

MAX: Ugh. Gross. No. OK. I'll shut up.

He rolls another cigarette for himself.

NATALIE: Thank you. It's just – I loved him. I really did. For him though, I just happened to be the girl who came along at the right time, with the right education, job, appearance … I could've been anyone! You know, I asked him once why he loved me.

Max shakes his head.

NATALIE: He basically recited my CV at me. And it's a pretty shitty CV!

MAX: OK. I have to say something! Sorry! But Natalie, geez! Why on earth are you still with him?!

NATALIE: (Jokes) Low self-esteem?

MAX: Seriously though. Why don't you just leave?!

NATALIE: I'm guess I'm scared. Have you ever looked at the numbers? Like really looked? There's 66 million people in the UK. 50.9% of those are married, another 11.7% cohabiting. Of the remaining single people, 5 to 7% are gay, and then there's race! Only 0.7% of people in the UK are Chinese, and only 9% of the rest are likely to enter inter-ethnic relationships. Divide what's left in half – if you count the gender ratio as 50/50 – and that leaves roughly 800,000 straight or bi men who'd be potentially into dating Chinese women. Oh, and that covers the very generous age range of 18 to 90.

MAX: 800,000? That doesn't sound so bad.

NATALIE: You know what that number would be for you? 7.6 million.

MAX: Well, now. I mean, I'm a bit more selective than 18 to 90. I like older women. 81 year olds. I mean, the free bus pass alone....

NATALIE: (Laughs) I'm serious! And think about the fact that it's the whole UK we're covering! I mean, when you factor in geography, interests, chemistry....

MAX: Attraction?

Natalie and Max suddenly get self-conscious and break eye-contact.

MAX: So, how did you –?

NATALIE: I made a spreadsheet.

MAX: (Laughs) You're a freak! You know that, right?

Max's laugh is infectious and Natalie can't help but laugh at herself too. Her smile fades as her eyes fall on the rabbit cage.

NATALIE: (Sighs) … I don't know if I can do it.

MAX: Listen to me, Natalie. You're more than your shitty CV. You're kind, you're funny and.... You know when I started here, the number one thing people said to me? OK, maybe not number one. I mean, there was a lot of "Who are you? Can I see your ID?" but a very close second was "Go ask Nat."

NATALIE: Those bastards.

MAX: No! It was because everyone knew you'd stop whatever you were doing to help out the new guy. You're just a wonderful person. We all see that, and if Tom doesn't, then he doesn't deserve you!

NATALIE: Max –

MAX: And I know I should just shut my stupid mouth while I'm ahead, but fuck it! Natalie, I like you. I've liked you since the moment I walked through that door8weeksago,andIknowit'sasurprise.I'mprettygoodathidingmyemotions–

Natalie opens her mouth to disagree.

MAX: And I know you think I'm too young, but you're wrong! There's that rule about never dating someone less than half your age plus 7. Well, half your age plus 7 is 24, so I pass! You trust numbers, so trust that! Trust yourself! You can leave him. Fuck the odds! He doesn't appreciate you and you deserve better! And I'm not saying that I'm better – I mean, I roll shit cigarettes and I talk too fucking much, but I just – I like you, Natalie. I like you. And please say something because I don't think I can stop this liquid shit pouring out of my mouth right now.

NATALIE: … I meant I didn't know if I could go through with killing 533955.

MAX: Ah. Well. He probably doesn't appreciate you enough either. Right. If you'll excuse me, I'm just going to sit here filled with self-loathing, and pray for the ground to swallow me up.

Max buries his head in his hands. Natalie tactfully lets him be. She strokes the rabbit in the cage.

NATALIE: You know, I've been taking care of 533955 for so long – feeding and handling him every day – it just seems wrong now for me to be the person to kill him.

Max suddenly straightens up.

MAX: I can do it.

NATALIE: What?

MAX: I can give 533955 the overdose of anaesthetic.

NATALIE: You don't have to do that.

MAX: I do. It's the least I can do after that appalling display back there. Here. Give me the syringe.

NATALIE: Have you done this before?

MAX: Yes. Of course. During training. On a dead one. (Hesitates) Maybe I should just read your notes first?

Natalie hands him her lab book. He deliberately takes his time.

MAX: OK. 533955. Age 335. Weight: 1.2. Disease progression: 300 days. Termination: Day 301. (Hesitates again) Look, what would happen, hypothetically, if we just didn't –?

Natalie grabs the syringe from him and jabs it in.

MAX: Shit! You just plunged that right in there! You Pulp Fictioned that rabbit!
NATALIE: (Horrified) Oh God! I did it! (Tearfully stroking the dying rabbit) Shh. It's OK, 533955. I'm here. I'm sorry. I'm so sorry.
MAX: (Quietly) Hey. You said yourself he'd only suffer if you didn't. It's better this way. You did the right thing.
NATALIE: Did I though?

They look into each other's eyes for a long beat.

NATALIE: (Softly) Brown eyes. He has brown eyes. Only 22% of the UK population have brown eyes....

The moment is broken by the sound of Natalie's phone. She reaches for it, but Max takes her hand.

MAX: Don't.
NATALIE: But, Tom –
MAX: You can do this, Natalie.
NATALIE: What if I can't?
MAX: Let me help you.

Natalie looks down at his hand on hers.

NATALIE: I'm 34.
MAX: It's just a number.

She pulls her hand away.

NATALIE: It's not! There's so much you haven't gone through! So much you need to see and experience, and –
MAX: How do you know I haven't? Get to know me! Give me a chance! It's just a number.
NATALIE: But numbers mean things! They're units – measures! There's orders and systems and –!

He steps closer to her. Natalie stops talking, her entire concentration taken by his near proximity.

MAX: I know you can feel this. Stop counting for once and just feel.
NATALIE: (To audience) Pulse rate 74, 82, 88, 97...

He takes her hand and puts it over his heart.

NATALIE: ... 102 ... 108 ... (Small gasp) The same. Our heartbeats are the same.
MAX: They're numbers, Natalie. They're just numbers.

Their lips almost touch. Natalie stops.

NATALIE: Nope! I can't. The third *Lord of the Rings* came out in cinemas when you were 10! 10!

Max sighs in disappointment.

NATALIE: I'm sorry. Hey. There's 7.6 million more fish in the sea?
MAX: Minus 1. Well, could I ask for just one thing?
NATALIE: What's that?

He hits play on his phone. Music plays.

MAX: Dance with me.
NATALIE: I don't know how!

He takes her hands, leading her to the music.

NATALIE: (Counts to the beat) 1 2 3 ... 1 2 3 ... 1 ... 2 ...

Max twirls her.

NATALIE: (Laughs)

As they continue to dance, her counting slowly stops and soon all we hear is the music.

Ends.

Afterword

Joanne Lau

The line "They're just numbers, really. Our lives, I mean." just popped into my head one day. I didn't know how I'd use it or what I'd flesh it out as, but it made such an impression that I emailed it to myself. I've still got the email. It's dated 16 July 2014. Fast forward to 17 December 2017. I was sitting around my parents' house sipping sloe gin and self-pity when a writer friend of mine sent me an opportunity for female BAME writers to submit a short play around the theme "Other Loves in Crisis". It looked fantastic but there was only one problem – I had nothing to say about love, in or out of crisis. I was single and miserable, and my heart was cold and dead. Still, an opportunity's an opportunity, so I wandered around the next few weeks whinging to friends and colleagues about the theme until one of them kindly and gently pointed out to me that I'd just come out of a nine-year relationship (hence the cold, dead heart and crawl back home to my parents) so probably had quite lot to say about "loves in crisis".

I think my response was to blow a raspberry, then run away shouting, "No, YOU'RE in denial!" because I'm classy and mature like that. And so I found myself stuck on a long train journey, staring out the window and contemplating what a mess my life was when suddenly that phrase popped back in my head "They're just numbers, really. Our lives, I mean." I took out my phone, found the email, hit reply and the dialogue just came vomiting out. Yup. I wrote the whole thing on my dinky little iPhone. It overheated a few times, so I'd have to wave it around desperately praying it didn't delete what I'd just written, but I just couldn't stop until I'd gotten it all out. When we finally pulled into London Marylebone that night, I had my complete first draft. I also like to think I had the first, very faint stirrings of a heartbeat again.

Part III

Isn't she lovely, made of love …

8   *Of Things Unsaid*

Jasmin Mandi-Ghomi

Characters

YASI, *early/mid-twenties, Iranian, short hair.*
ALICE, *early/mid-twenties, YASI's fiancée, any ethnicity.*
AFSI, *forties, Iranian, YASI's mother, speaks good English but has an Iranian accent.*

Notes

(–) at the end of a line indicates being cut off.
(…) indicates where speech trails off.
(Beat) indicates a brief break in the dialogue.
(Silence) indicates the point at which characters do not know what to say next, or how to say it.
This script contains some basic Iranian that is translated below.
Salam – hello.
Khalid khoobi – how are you?
Khoobam – I am well.
Bebakhshid – sorry.
Joon/azizam – darling.
Jendeh – slut (a very offensive term).
A chador is a type of hijab that is popular amongst Shi'a Muslim women. It is a big piece of fabric that is wrapped around the head and body but leaves the face exposed.

Original production details

Of Things Unsaid was commissioned and produced by Little Pieces of Gold at Southwark Playhouse on 23 September 2018.

The cast was as follows:

AFSI	Lanna Joffrey
ALICE	Kerry Fitzgerald
YASI	Peyvand Sadeghian
Director:	Laura Kressly

A living room in London. There are a few pot plants and three chairs. Alice is sat down and reading a book.

YASI: (From offstage) Where are the tomatoes?
ALICE: The what?
YASI: (From offstage) The tomatoes?
ALICE: The what?

Yasi enters.

YASI: I said where are the tomatoes?
ALICE: They're in the bread bin.
YASI: What?
ALICE: They're in the fridge! Where else would they be?
YASI: They're not there.
ALICE: That means we don't have any.
YASI: We must do! I bought some yesterday.
ALICE: We made salad last night....
YASI: Great! What do I do now?
ALICE: You could make something else?
YASI: You are the complete opposite of helpful.

Yasi moves to walk offstage.

ALICE: Yasi, wait....
YASI: I was making her favourite meal! It was meant to sweeten her up. I can't even do that right.
ALICE: Why don't I go out and get some more tomatoes for you?
YASI: I wouldn't want to put you out as you're obviously so very busy.
ALICE: Come on, you know I want today to go as smoothly as possible. I just don't think that a lack of tomatoes will swing it either way.
YASI: You obviously know very little about the Iranian people. Food is everything to us.
ALICE: Well you're everything to me so if you want me to go and get tomatoes then I will.
YASI: That was the corniest thing you've ever said.
ALICE: Did it make you feel better though?
YASI: Maybe a little bit.
ALICE: Then it was worth it.

They kiss but Yasi abruptly pulls out of it.

YASI: Wait, where's Jasper?
ALICE: Outside, I think. Why?

YASI: Would temporarily bordering up the cat flap count as animal cruelty?

ALICE: Yeah, probably. Plus, he'll just sit and scratch at the front door and I only repainted it last month. What are you talking about?

YASI: Mum hates cats.

ALICE: Is there anything that your mother likes?

YASI: Tomatoes, but apparently we're out of those.

ALICE: There must be some somewhere. Let me go and have a look. Please don't border up the cat flap while I'm gone.

Alice exits into the offstage kitchen. Yasi is alone on stage, she looks out into the audience as if she's looking into a mirror and nervously combs through her hair. A few moments pass.
Alice enters.

ALICE: I found the tomatoes.

YASI: What? Where?

ALICE: In the fridge, where I said they would be.

YASI: Mashallah, thank you Jesus.

ALICE: I just put them in the pot. They are simmering as we speak.

YASI: You are an angel.

ALICE: I know.

Beat. Yasi runs a hand through her hair.

ALICE: Your hair looks great.

YASI: I'm not sure anymore....

ALICE: It really suits you, I promise.

YASI: What is my Mum going to think?

ALICE: I think she will have more to worry about than your hair.

YASI: Don't say that. I'm not even sure that we're making the right choice anymore.

ALICE: To get married?

YASI: To tell her that we are getting married.

ALICE: You know your mother better than anyone. You know what she can handle and what she can't.

YASI: I'm starting to regret ever having asked her to come round.

ALICE: Look, Yasi, this is entirely your decision to make – I'm not going to force you to come out to her. What I will say is that I think she deserves the chance to know you. She deserves the chance to be involved in the wedding of her daughter. If she throws it back in your face then it's her loss, but if you don't even give her a chance then it's yours.

YASI: When did you get so smart?

ALICE: I've got a degree, I'll have you know.

YASI: You got a third.

ALICE: Still counts as a degree though! Still counts.

Knock on the door.

YASI: Oh god. Should I put a headscarf on?
ALICE: Why would you put a headscarf on?
YASI: It'll look more modest.
ALICE: You gave up the hijab when you were 16.
YASI: Maybe I want to take it up again?
ALICE: There are only women here, you maniac. Just answer the door.

Another knock.

YASI: I can't!
ALICE: Stop panicking. Take a deep breath and smile. That's it. Now, go and answer the door.

Yasi paints a smile on her face and pulls the door open. Afsi, her mother, is waiting on the doorstep in a chador.

YASI: Maman!
AFSI: Salam Yasi joon. Khalid khoobi?
YASI: Khoobam maman. Bebakhshid, can we speak English please? For Alice.
AFSI: Alice, of course. How are you, honey?
ALICE: I'm good, thanks, Mrs Afsi.
AFSI: Aren't you two getting a little old to be flatmates now? You're not in university anymore. Maybe it's time you both think about getting your own houses.

Beat.

ALICE: Well, this way we save on the rent.
AFSI: Of course. Now Yasi, let me look at you properly. You're too thin, are you eating enough? Have you been eating rice? Do I need to make rice for you? Wait … (Beat) Your hair. Where is your hair? Your beautiful hair! (Afsi forcibly spins Yasi round). I thought you'd put it up! It's gone, it's completely gone. I think I need to sit down.
ALICE: Why don't I take your chador and make us some tea?
AFSI: Yes, I need tea. Thank you, Alice. Why do you shock me like this, Yasi?

Alice takes the chador and exits into the kitchen, leaving Yasi and Afsi alone. They both sit down in silence. A moment.

YASI: So, about the hair –
AFSI: Why do you always do this to me? You give me no warning. You should tell me these things.
YASI: It's just hair, Maman.

AFSI: There is nothing 'just' about your hair, Yasi. It was so long and beautiful. Everybody envied your hair. Now you look like a boy.

YASI: It's just short! That doesn't automatically mean I look like a boy.

AFSI: Girls have long hair.

YASI: Not always. Not all women have long hair. What about Audrey Hepburn?

AFSI: She had a lovely face.

YASI: And I don't have a lovely face?

AFSI: You have a face that needs long hair.

YASI: I can do what I want with my hair.

AFSI: You stopped wearing the hijab so that you could show off your hair and this is what you do to it?

YASI: I stopped wearing the hijab because I didn't want to wear it anymore.

AFSI: All so you could shave yourself bald.

YASI: How am I bald? How is this bald?!

Alice enters with three cups of tea and some biscuits on a tray.

ALICE: Tea.

An awkward silence blossoms between them all.

ALICE: Mrs Afsi, please help yourself to some biscuits.

AFSI: Thank you, honey.

Silence.

YASI: How's Baba?

AFSI: Your father? How would I know? I haven't seen him for six months.

YASI: He said that you were getting on better when he last phoned.

AFSI: That man is a compulsive liar. He lies about everything. Don't trust a word he says.

YASI: He's not that bad –

AFSI: He said he was working late when really he was with that jendeh –

YASI: Maman, please don't use that word –

AFSI: That … that … what's the English word? Slut! That slut!

YASI: Nothing happened between them, Maman. They were just colleagues.

AFSI: And who told you that? Him! The compulsive liar. (Turns to Alice) Never get married. It's a scam.

ALICE: I don't believe that.

AFSI: You don't believe it because you've never done it. It only ever ends in heartbreak. You don't need a husband!

ALICE: Now that I can get on board with.

AFSI: I'm thinking of finding myself a nice young man instead.

YASI: Excuse me?

AFSI: Your auntie was telling me all about this thing you can get on your phone

and it finds men for you. You put up a picture and then they all start talking
to you. I think I might try it out.

YASI: Are you talking about Tinder?

AFSI: Tinder! Yes. That's it.

YASI: Maman, you are not downloading Tinder.

AFSI: Why not?

YASI: You're 47.

AFSI: So what? Young men like older women now. I might even find myself a
young white man. Imagine that.

YASI: Please stop talking.

AFSI: You should try it out, Yasi. You might meet someone.

YASI: I promise you that nobody I want to meet is on Tinder.

AFSI: Now that is just unfair. From what your auntie said it sounds like it is full
of lovely young men who like to send you pictures.

YASI: Can we just stop talking about Tinder?

AFSI: What about you, Alice? Do you have a gentleman to entertain you yet?

ALICE: Well … there is someone.…

Yasi shoots Alice a warning look.

AFSI: Tell me everything!

ALICE: Well, it's been going on for quite a while now and –

YASI: Maman, do you want more tea?

AFSI: My cup is still full. Alice, what were you saying?

ALICE: Nothing, apparently.

AFSI: Don't let Yasi interrupt you. She's always been so bossy.

ALICE: Don't worry about it. It was nothing.

AFSI: (To Yasi) Look what you've done now.

YASI: I haven't done anything. I was just offering you some more tea.

AFSI: Alice, please go on.

An awkward silence.

ALICE: Well –

YASI: We're getting married.

AFSI: What?

YASI: Alice and I, we're getting married.

AFSI: To – to who?

YASI: To each other.

Silence.

YASI: Maman, I –

AFSI: Finally

YASI: Finally?

AFSI: Finally! It only took you six years to tell me.

YASI: Wait, I'm confused.

ALICE: You knew?

AFSI: Of course I knew. Look at all of these pot plants.

YASI: Pot plants don't make us gay!

AFSI: You made a home. That's how I knew.

YASI: Why didn't you say anything?

AFSI: I wanted to see how long it would take for you to tell me.

YASI: So all that just now, about Tinder and finding a man, you were playing us?

AFSI: Of course I was. Why would I download Tinder? Too many willies on there for me.

YASI: Please never say that again in your life.

AFSI: Why did it take you until you were planning a wedding to tell me?! All this time and now you spring a wedding on me.

YASI: I was worried that you'd hate me.

AFSI: My crazy child. Why would I hate you?

YASI: Come on, Maman, I know it's haram.

AFSI: Yasi, how many times have you read the Qu'ran?

Beat.

YASI: None.

AFSI: And how many times have I read the Qu'ran?

YASI: Five?

AFSI: Seven, actually. After seven thorough readings I can safely say, without a doubt, that love is not haram.

YASI: But they kill people for this in Iran.

AFSI: I know, azizam. There are lots of things wrong with this world. There are lots of things wrong about the way people think and what people believe but there is nothing wrong with my little girl … with my girls.

Afsi holds the hands of both Yasi and Alice.

YASI: What will Baba say?

AFSI: You leave your father to me. He'll come around.

A moment.

AFSI: I should say congratulations. You'll both make beautiful brides. (To Yasi) You'd be even more beautiful if you grew your hair back.

YASI: Maman –

AFSI: I'm just saying that long hair would look nicer under a veil.

YASI: I'm keeping the short hair.

AFSI: Fine, but please promise me one thing?

YASI: Alright.

AFSI: There will be babies. I don't care how you do it but I want Grandchildren as soon as possible.

YASI: It's a bit soon for that –

ALICE: I think we can do that for you, Mrs Afsi.

AFSI: Please, call me Maman.

ALICE: Okay, Maman.

AFSI: Now, you promised me food.

ALICE: We've made your favourite rice!

AFSI: Great. We should start planning the wedding over dinner. There better be tomatoes!

Ends.

Afterword

Jasmin Mandi-Ghomi

This piece was born out of a desire to write something happy. Growing up, I barely ever saw Islamic people portrayed on stage and, if I did, the characters were almost always in a dark and desperate situation. *Of Things Unsaid* is my rebellion against that. It begins happy and it ends happy. It is merely the story of a mother and daughter trying to navigate their way through their lives together. The mother/daughter dynamic is one I have always wanted to explore and the idea of a young Iranian woman coming out to her religious mother felt like the perfect way to do that. There are all sorts of family connections in this piece and all of them are both vital and valid. Mostly, I just wanted to show that Islam is a religion of peace and love. Islamic women, no matter their ethnicity, age or sexual orientation, deserve to be seen and heard on stage.

9 *Stopcock*

Christine Robertson

Characters

MJ, *early twenties. Low-key anxious, uses humour as defence.*
GINA, *late fifties. Deadpan professional* [NB. This performer also plays NURSE].
LUKE, *mid-twenties. Warm and supportive, if a little out of his depth.*

Notes

(/) marks the point where the immediately following dialogue interrupts.
(–) at the end of a line indicates being cut off.
(…) at the end of a speech means it trails off. On its own it indicates a pressure or expectation to speak.
(Pause) indicates where there is a thought process happening.

Original production details

Stopcock was commissioned and produced by Little Pieces of Gold at Southwark Playhouse on 24 September 2017.

The cast was as follows:

MJ	Adele James
GINA	Michelle Greenidge
LUKE	Anyebe Godwin
Director:	Rebekah Murrell

Scene One

MJ sits opposite Gina in a therapy session. Gina holds a 'Pocket Pussy' sex toy with moulded rubber 'vagina' opening towards MJ. MJ is grimacing.

MJ: I can't put my finger in that; I'm sorry.
GINA: What's wrong?

MJ: Everything about this situation is deeply unsexy. No offence.

GINA: This is about the biology of your vagina and helping you understand it. It's not meant to be sexy.

MJ: How many other fingers have been in that thing? It's just fingers that go in there, right?

GINA: It's just fingers.

MJ stares at it for a bit, thinking.

MJ: But it's not, like, designed for fingers though, is it?

GINA: It's designed to be penetrated. By what is secondary. Take your time.

MJ stares at it a little longer.

MJ: This is hard, man. I can't go there.

GINA: What don't you like about it?

MJ: Look at it, it's gross.

GINA: You think vaginas are gross?

MJ: Doesn't everyone that comes here?

GINA: No. What is it about vaginas that you find gross?

MJ: I know they give life and they're the source of all our power or whatever but they're just … weird.

GINA: So you've used "gross" and "weird". Can you elaborate on either?

MJ: I don't know; it's just like, a hole. Guarded by flaps. It's confusing.

GINA: 'Confusing' is quite different to "gross" and "weird".

MJ: Why is this now GCSE English?

GINA: If we can understand why this repulses you –

MJ: I didn't say "repulse".

GINA: Does it not repulse you?

MJ: (Pause) It does a little bit, yeah.

GINA: Then I can help you overcome your reluctance to penetrate it. What do you find gross, weird and confusing about this?

MJ: You piss from it daily. You bleed from it monthly. Random discharge, sweat, hair. Who wants to touch that?

GINA: OK, well this is just rubber. Nothing in it but air look.

She squeezes air from it towards MJ's face – MJ recoils.

MJ: Ugh.

GINA: In your own time.

MJ takes a big breath and slowly moves a finger towards it – pulls it back suddenly.

MJ: Is this a trap? Are you gonna clamp my finger when I put it in there?

GINA: It's not a trap.

MJ: Cause that would be incredibly cruel. And unprofessional.

GINA: I'm not setting you up, MJ. No pranks, no sudden moves; I'm just going to hold it still until you're ready.

After some deep breaths and psyching up, MJ pushes her finger into the 'opening'. She and Gina sit silently, still.

GINA: How do you feel?

Gina freezes as MJ addresses the audience.

MJ: I mean … we look ridiculous.

She removes her finger and gags.

MJ: She kind of sprang that on me; I just need a minute to congratulate myself for doing that before I get back into it.

MJ: I know how that looked. I knew it was possible, sticking my finger in that thing. I knew it was physically possible. But I'm not here for the physical. I'm here for the psychosexual. Yeah, it's a word. It sounds like you're nuts in bed – "she's a terrifying lover, borderline psychosexual." Or a sub-genre of '90s Hollywood erotica – "Psychosexual thriller Rough Silk is a return to form for Courtney Cox. Three stars."

MJ: Yeah no it doesn't mean either of those things. Psychosexual means a woman old enough to be your mum asks you to finger a rubber vagina, and your instinct to scoff at the absurdity of it is only trumped by the shock that you don't actually know if you can do it.

MJ: But I did it.

MJ: And that's a big deal for me. But I have to high-five you privately about it because successfully fingering a rubber vagina is not the kind of big deal that my friends and family will understand, or even want to hear. Maybe that's unfair on them but I'm comfortable with that assumption. They assume you're sexually active when you're in a relationship and I'm comfortable with that assumption too.

MJ: OK, I don't know what the rules are about me talking to you like this and if it's eating into my hour long appointment –

GINA: (Still frozen) It is.

MJ: – oh it is, OK.

She returns to sit opposite Gina. Realises she needs to reinsert her finger.

MJ: Hmmm. Yeah. OK, I've not thought this through. Maybe I'll just....

MJ knocks the Pocket Pussy out of Gina's hand, "unfreezing" Gina.

MJ: (To Gina) Sorry, I had to pull out.

GINA: Well done. How did it feel?

MJ: Like I've earned the rest of the day off?

GINA: Well done. For next week, I'd like you to try slipping a finger in at home.

MJ: Don't say "slipping". It sounds like a ruse, or an accident.

GINA: You could pop a finger in in the bath if that makes it easier.

MJ: OK, is the bath full or am I like, just sat in a dry tub?

Gina raises an eyebrow, losing her patience.

MJ: Could I get my boyfriend to put his finger in?

GINA: It's important you get to know how your body feels. We've talked about the anticipation of pain but I also think your vaginismus partly stems from unfamiliarity with your own vagina.

MJ looks distressed.

GINA: MJ – think about what you want to achieve by the end of therapy. Think about all the times vaginismus has prevented you from doing certain things.

MJ: I kicked a nurse in the face at a smear test.

GINA: Fantastic; imagine being able to have a smear test without kicking a nurse in the face.

MJ: Every two years I buy a box of tampons, try and insert one, have a meltdown and give the rest of the box to a homeless shelter.

GINA: OK; imagine being able to keep the next box because you're finally able to use them.

MJ: What about the homeless shelter?

GINA: Stop deflecting, MJ. What else do you want to achieve?

MJ: I want the confidence to land on a hard cock from a great height, like a gymnast might.

GINA: Maybe just imagine being able to lower yourself gently onto a hard cock from a sensible height to begin with.

MJ: I can't imagine doing any of this to be honest.

Gina hands MJ a hardback book that's just photos of vaginas.

GINA: Here. If placing a finger in your vagina proves difficult, then I'd like you to take a leisurely look through this book – and then at your own vagina in a mirror.

MJ flicks through the book quickly, anxiously.

MJ: Wait, is this just all vaginas? This book is my nightmare.

GINA: It's important to understand that vaginas can all look wildly different.

MJ: I'm happy to take your word for it.

Gina gets a hand mirror.

GINA: When it comes to examining yourself in a mirror, this position gives you a good view....

Gina spreads her legs and holds a mirror in front of her navy polyester crotch. MJ is trying not to react.

MJ: Uh-huh ...
GINA: Or you could kneel on the floor and place it underneath you –

Gina starts to heft herself off her seat.

MJ: Ah, that's OK. I'm sure I can work out which angle's best.
GINA: Do you want to borrow this mirror?
MJ: I don't know.... How many other vaginas have looked in it?

Scene Two

That evening, MJ and her boyfriend Luke are on her bed, leafing through the book – the hand mirror on the bedside table.

MJ: Imagine project managing this book. "Yeah hi, I'm producing a book of vaginas. No, more like a coffee table book. Just a fuck-load of vaginas, tastefully shot. No text. Yeah, could I get a quote on some paper stock? I'm thinking, coated, silk finish?"
LUKE: They become quite abstract after a while, don't they? When you've looked at them page after page. They lose their meaning. They're not vaginas anymore. They're like ambitious ... sea creatures.

MJ puts the book down hurriedly, glad it's over.

MJ: OK, I've scraped a pass on the theory. Now I've gotta get through the practical.

MJ squirts some lube onto her forefinger, lays down, spreads her legs and starts some deep breathing. Luke opens Spotify on his phone.

LUKE: I compiled a playlist for the occasion.
MJ: The occasion of fingering myself?
LUKE: Yeah.

MJ gets a shock as a blast of "Open Up!" by Leftfield ft. John Lydon plays way too loud. Luke does rave hands, grinning.

MJ: (Scowling) Oh my god!

Luke cuts the music off. MJ just about sees the funny side of it.

LUKE: Bit of fun.

MJ: I don't know how to get in the zone for this.

LUKE: Would it help to think of really wide, cavernous spaces? Like when you think about waterfalls to help you have a piss?

MJ: I want to say no?

LUKE: C'mon, let's try.

MJ: OK but try and be relaxing with it.

Luke strokes her head gently, while MJ closes her eyes and tries to relax.

LUKE: The Grand Canyon ... An Albatross's wingspan ... The Joker's smile, that's wide isn't it ... Um ... I've gone blank, sorry. Did any of those help?

MJ: Strangely no.

LUKE: Sorry, I should've prepped that better.

MJ: Let's try the hand mirror.

Luke nabs the mirror and holds it in front of her face – she laughs.

MJ: Not my face, my ... part.

LUKE: "Part" – it's your pussy.

MJ: Don't say "pussy." It makes me think of mangy alley cats.

LUKE: Blimey, you really don't like vaginas do you?

MJ: I know. I'm sorry. I'm trying.

Luke places the hand mirror in front of MJ's vagina. She sits up slightly to get a view – though she takes a bit too long laying her eyes on her reflection.

LUKE: Nice, right?

MJ: Ugh. Is it?

LUKE: Yeah. Knockout.

MJ: I suppose it wouldn't look out of place in the book....

LUKE: That's the spirit. Right, ready for Operation: Finger Your Hole?

MJ: Nice pillow talk, babe. OK, OK.... Will you help me guide it in?

MJ starts to psych herself up – deep breaths. Luke lies next to her and gently helps guide her finger in.

MJ: Is this right?

LUKE: That's it.

MJ: Ah, I don't like it.

LUKE: It's OK. There's no rush. Just breathe slowly. Relax your shoulders.

MJ: (Deep breath) Jeez, I don't even realise I was that tense.

MJ resumes trying. A few more deep breaths. Eventually she turns to the audience.

MJ: I already know this won't work. It won't. The conditions aren't right. I know how that sounds. Fussy, deflective. But conditions are crucial. I went for a smear test once. I'd explained I was nervous and she was very understanding ... but there's understanding and there's –

Nurse swoops in, starts fussing over MJ.

NURSE: That's it, you get comfy for me sweetheart. You're in charge, OK? You're in charge. You're the car and I'm the mechanic. I'm here to service you, so whatever you need, you just tell me.

MJ: (To audience) How do I ask a perfectly lovely nurse who's going out of her way to help me relax, to just ... dial it down a bit? I can't do that, I don't want to crush her confidence too. At least one of us needs confidence in this scenario. (To nurse) I'm sorry I couldn't do it that day. Please don't think you failed. I appreciate you trying.

NURSE: It's alright sweetheart. I'm just relieved you didn't kick me in the face like my colleague Karen had once. You're in charge, remember. You're the boss.

Exit Nurse. MJ looks at ("frozen") Luke.

MJ: He's trying to help too. And he's perfect. And it's nothing he's done that means I can't do this right now. But the conditions aren't right. The conditions up here I mean (taps head). I only just fingered a rubber vagina today, I can't go crashing into my own flesh vagina like a hungry hippo yet. Is there a penetrative equivalent of running before you can walk? I don't know. Anyway, I still don't know the rules about talking to you. No-one's told me and I don't know who to ask.

She gets back into position.

MJ: Time to put us both out of our misery.

MJ's deep breaths become increasingly frustrated.

MJ: I'm sorry. I'm sorry ... It's not working. I'm sorry, it's not happening.

MJ hides her face in shame. Luke comforts her.

LUKE: Hey, it's OK. We'll get there.

MJ: What if we don't? What if I don't? This might be it for me.

LUKE: Then we just go really hard on oral. Let our tongues get thick and hench.

MJ laugh-cries.

MJ: (Quietly) You know you can bail anytime.

LUKE: What do you mean?

MJ: You're either incredibly patient, desperate to get laid, or both.

LUKE: Or I could just really like you.

MJ: You didn't sign up for this though.

LUKE: No-one knows what the hell they sign up for at the start.

MJ: We've been dating for three months and haven't had sex.

LUKE: But the other stuff we're doing is fun. And when we do finally have some deep pen – and we will, 'cause I believe in you – we'll have the excitement of starting all over again. All new things to try. If anything, we're extending our sex life by at least three months.

MJ: You've given this a lot of thought.

LUKE: I'm a big thinker. That's my embarrassing problem.

MJ: Thanks for opting in. I'm terrified, mortified and feeling very undignified. And I don't know how it'll pan out but … I'm glad it's with you.

They kiss. Lights dim to blackout over "Let's Talk About Sex" by Salt-N-Pepa.

Ends.

Afterword

Christine Robertson

I remember hearing "No sex please, we're British" occasionally as a girl and always finding it funny – despite not fully getting the reference. Many years later, having recently sat opposite a stony-faced sex therapist and struggled to finger a rubber vagina at her request, it dawned on me that our cultural unease with talking about sex was manifesting in a lot of needless shame and dysfunction. *Stopcock* is my attempt to ease the dread, celebrate candour and help normalise conversation about sex.

Good luck!

Part IV

Aping the patriarchy

10 *The Petal and The Orchid*

Clare Joy Langford and Gabrielle Curtis

Characters

KATHRYN, *about 40, neatly turned out, professional. Kathryn is the coordinating executive of the charity MissEducation. A strong, fair and impassioned worker, highly respected by her colleagues and seniors.*

LEONA, *about 30, presentable but relaxed in appearance. Leona is the project manager and key field worker on the Lesotho Community Development Project. Fiercely independent and hard-working, she copes well with the austerity that the job often demands. She has a tendency to put work above all else, often to the neglect of her personal life.*

Notes

(/) marks the point where the immediately following dialogue interrupts.

(–) at the end of a line indicates being cut off.

(…) at the end of a speech means it trails off. On its own it indicates a pressure or expectation to speak.

(Beat) indicates a brief break in the dialogue.

(Pause) indicates where there is a thought process happening.

Original production details

The Petal and The Orchid was commissioned and produced by Little Pieces of Gold at Southwark Playhouse on 4 February 2018.

The cast was as follows:

KATHRYN	Marilii Saar
LEONA	Lydia Bakelmun
Director:	Brigitte Adela

Offices of MISSEDUCATION, a medium-sized charity organisation in Islington, London, specialising in the safeguarding, education and empowerment of young girls and women – with a particular focus on prevention of and protection from sex crimes and abuse.

Friday afternoon, 4pm. Typical office hubbub: the clatter of keyboards, photocopiers and the like; hum of noise as people chat and start to wind down for the weekend.

Lights up, Kathryn's office: simple, very organised. A large clock is ticking on the wall beside her desk. Another small ornate clock sits on her desk. Framed photographs from the Lesotho project are tastefully scattered on the walls. A small bookcase with a selective library, mostly feminism, African culture, education, etc. A couple of framed family photos are on the desk, alongside her phone and computer.

Two matching potted flowers (orchids) sit on either side of the desk.

Kathryn sits at her desk working, glancing up only occasionally to look at the clock. She gets up to examine the flowers and gives each of them a spray. Sits back down when satisfied they are sufficiently watered. 4pm precisely. A knock at the door.

KATHRYN: Come in.

Leona enters, somewhat uneasy. She's a confident woman but is aware of Kathryn's professional superiority and that the following conversation may be a difficult one.

LEONA: Hi Kathryn … now still a good time?
KATHRYN: Sure. Take a seat.

Leona closes the door behind her and sits down.

KATHRYN: How are you?
LEONA: Good – busy, but good. How are you?
KATHRYN: Yeah, fine, just trying to tie things up before the weekend – Alan's parents are coming down.
LEONA: Oh nice! Well thanks for agreeing to meet me. I know you're up the walls … but I wanted to have a quick chat about the trip.
KATHRYN: Yes, I got your email … let me just bring it up....

Kathryn consults emails on her computer.

KATHRYN: (Without looking up) Congratulations by the way.... It seems to be going really well.
LEONA: Thanks, it is.
KATHRYN: David is delighted with what you're doing.
LEONA: Oh great, I'm glad he's pleased. I mean there's always more to do but we're making progress. It seems like they're getting used to having us around.
KATHRYN: (Still looking through emails) I think he'll be even more impressed when he actually sees it for himself....

Leona flinches, looks uncomfortable.

KATHRYN: Why is there so much junk in here? … One of these days I'll get around to … right, there it is … let me just have a quick re-read.…

Kathryn quickly skims through, Leona sits in silence until Kathryn looks up.

KATHRYN: Ah that was it … You don't think David should come on the trip?

LEONA: Yeah, like I was saying, it's taken a long time to establish a connection with the people out there, and finally it's paying off – they're starting to respect me. I'm just concerned that if I arrive out there with a man … a man like David … well … there's this tendency to defer to men, to talk over a woman's head.

KATHRYN: Yes, they do the same here.

LEONA: Right, well, so imagine Islington times 100.… It's a very small traditional community; as soon as they have a man to communicate with, especially a certain type of man, the women around them become invisible – that's just how it is. Look, don't get me wrong – I think David is great, he's charismatic, he's a fantastic businessman, he's a titan of efficiency … but I think him being there might prove a bit of a distraction to what we're trying to achieve. I just don't want to, you know, upset the mango cart.…

Kathryn laughs.

KATHRYN: Ok, I see what you're saying; he is quite a presence. But I wouldn't worry about him trying to impose. He'll take one look at the modest conditions of your camp, and as soon as he's taken a few "Mother Teresa" style selfies, he'll hotfoot it to The Hilton. He'll probably spend the rest of the trip on a safari! Your mango carts will be safe.

LEONA: Yes … but … what if he doesn't? What if he decides he wants to "get involved", relive his gap year.…

KATHRYN: Well, we'll cross that bridge when we come to it. Anyway, come on, you can hold your own against David … you'll run rings around him.

LEONA: I can promise you I will be talked through if he is there.

KATHRYN: (Beginning to lose patience) And if you are? Does it really matter? Let him have a bit of the limelight if he wants it. Your job is to lead your team, keep things moving and see the project through.

LEONA: I don't think you quite understand.

KATHRYN: I do understand but what do you want me to do? David wants to go, I've given it a green light and you haven't given me sufficient reason to backtrack. I appreciate your frustrations but he writes the cheques so if he wants to go, he goes.

LEONA: This isn't some executive schmoozing event at the Dorchester; this is work on the ground – building bridges, gaining trust.

KATHRYN: All of which he is very good at; they are transferable skills.

LEONA: Yeah, I'm just not sure how smoothly they transfer from Mayfair to Lesotho....

KATHRYN: (Dismissively) Alright Leona, well we can't all be "woman of the people" but we offer what we can.... You're going to have to find a way to manage this situation. Look, I think we're going to have to leave it there.

LEONA: He can't come –

Beat.

LEONA: I can't go out there with him, I can't be alone with him in a camp.

KATHRYN: What? Why not?

LEONA: I just can't.

KATHRYN: Leona what are you talking about?

LEONA: We have history.

KATHRYN: History? What do you mean?

LEONA: We had a relationship ... an affair.

KATHRYN: (Shocked) What?! When?

LEONA: I don't know ... it started about this time last year....

Beat.

KATHRYN: Is it over?

LEONA: Yes, God, yes.

KATHRYN: What the hell were you thinking?

LEONA: I don't know, I'm an idiot, it just happened.

Kathryn is visibly angered by this revelation. She despises personal matters getting in the way of work and is acutely aware that the key project manager getting involved with the chief patron could have serious ramifications for what the organisation is trying to achieve.

LEONA: He ... he is an incredibly magnetic man, we were spending a lot of time together ... I'm not excusing it....

KATHRYN: I'm glad you're not excusing it because I have zero interest in hearing excuses. The main thing is that it's over.

Beat.

KATHRYN: (Sensing Leona's unease) What?

LEONA: That's not it.... He ... we had an argument the last time we met.

KATHRYN: So?

LEONA: He got aggressive, very aggressive actually. I'd told him it was over, but he wasn't having it. He was angry that it hadn't ended on his terms I think. So he wanted to take something with him, have the final word. I didn't want a goodbye fuck, but he did. And what David wants, David gets.

KATHRYN: (Taken aback) Are you saying?

Leona nods.

KATHRYN: Are you sure?

Beat.

KATHRYN: Leona – I'm asking you to be absolutely sure. Because if there is any doubt in your mind.... Sometimes intimate situations can be ambiguous –

LEONA: Oh you can't be serious – I educate girls and women about their bodies, about self-worth, about violation … I do that every day of my life; We both know the difference between consent and rape. There is no ambiguity. Fucking hell!

Kathryn is now deeply conflicted. She is moved by Leona's obvious despair; rape and sexual abuse of any kind is abhorrent to her and diametrically at odds with her value system. However, she remains acutely aware of the potentially catastrophic consequences of this revelation.

KATHRYN: (More softly) When did this happen?

LEONA: About two months ago.

KATHRYN: Have you seen him since then?

LEONA: No, thank goodness.

KATHRYN: Why didn't you say anything to me at the time?

LEONA: I thought I could deal with it. And I didn't think I'd have to see again him face to face. I certainly didn't think we'd be cosying up in a tent! To be honest, I just wanted to forget it – the whole thing was, is, such a mess. I figured the best possible option was to try and get on with it. And I'm just about managing to do that, but now … well … I feel like I'm heading into the lion's enclosure, but without the four-wheel jeep to protect me.

KATHRYN: (With resignation) I'll talk to him. I'll convince him not to go out to Africa with you.

LEONA: What are you going to say?

KATHRYN: I'll think of something.

LEONA: I'm sorry … I do realise it's difficult.

KATHRYN: Just leave it with me.

LEONA: Right … is that it then?

KATHRYN: I think so.

LEONA: Ok, well, thanks for hearing me out – I'll leave you to it then.

Leona goes to leave.

KATHRYN: (Without looking up from her work) And Leona, try and conduct yourself with a little more propriety going forward. I have enough on my plate without having to deal with internal squabbles.

LEONA: "Internal squabbles"?

Leona turning back into the room and closing the door.

LEONA: This isn't a case of him taking too long replying to my emails! He raped me.

KATHRYN: Yes, I'm painfully aware of that.

LEONA: You know what? This isn't good enough.

KATHRYN: (Exasperated) What do you want now Leona?

LEONA: I've changed my mind, I want him to pay for what he's done.

KATHRYN: Five minutes ago you wanted him taken off the trip? Now what, you want his dick on a chopping board?

LEONA: You have absolutely no idea what the last few months have been like for me! How it's weighed on me, I feel sick all the time, I can't concentrate, I'm holding on by a thread! I want him to be held responsible.

KATHRYN: Leona when did this happen? Two months ago you said?

LEONA: About that.

KATHRYN: And, in your experience, how easy is it to prove a rape two months after the event? (Pause) Presuming the victim has no photographic evidence, which I assume you don't? (Pause) We're dealing with an accusation which has zero evidence against a man with whom you have admitted to having an extramarital relationship. You'd be lucky if he was even taken in for questioning.

LEONA: Isn't there something you can do? Internally?

KATHRYN: Yes, there is. I can call the chief patron of the organisation into the office which he pays to sustain, tell him that he has been accused not only of having an affair, but also of being a rapist. And I'll proceed to tell the man who is effectively your boss and my boss, that his services are no longer required. And that'll teach him, won't it? Of course the ripple effect will be quite far reaching. There will be repercussions for the few hundred young girls that we have worked tirelessly to protect from the most horrific abuses imaginable. But, we'll just chalk that down to collateral damage shall we?

LEONA: That's not fair.

KATHRYN: No, Leona, it's not fair but it is true.

LEONA: Don't do that, don't try and guilt me into dropping this.

KATHRYN: I have spent my life championing women's rights –

LEONA: Unless that woman happens to be a white middle class colleague –

KATHRYN: Unless that white middle class colleague is responsible for the protection of hundreds of young women and girls ten times more vulnerable than her. And, yes Leona, bizarrely, I do tend to care more for a twelve year old girl dragged screaming from her bed to become a child bride or to be gang raped than I do for a thirty-something year old woman who has been blessed with every possible opportunity she could have wanted. So, as much as it pains me to hierarchise rape, I am afraid the distinction in this case is screamingly obvious.

LEONA: I'm a human being – I made a mistake, that shouldn't take away my right to justice.

KATHRYN: I don't know what you expect me to do.

LEONA: What if we went to the press?

KATHRYN: Are you crazy? Are you trying to think up ways to make the situation even worse than it is? Why the hell would you want to go to the press?

LEONA: Well, what if I'm not the only one? What if he's done this before? If it goes public, other women might come forward.

KATHRYN: Oh great! From Bill Gates to Harvey Weinstein in one fell swoop.

LEONA: I'm not saying he's a predator; I'm saying I might not be the only one he's raped, And if I was to come forward –

KATHRYN: /Then what? Some gaggle of mistreated junior execs will come running behind you sighing with relief that they can finally pursue the justice they deserve?

LEONA: Yes actually. And if there are others, and they speak out, I will have a case and it will have to be investigated, right?

KATHRYN: (Reluctantly) Yes, Leona, then it would have to be investigated.

LEONA: Well that's it then. That's what I want to do.

KATHRYN: And then what? Onwards and upwards?

LEONA: You know I'm not that naive.

KATHRYN: I'm starting to wonder.... You go to the press with this – not only will the scandal reduce the entire organisation's reputation to tatters but every one of our personal lives will be scrutinised to the hills and splashed across the papers.... And don't think for one moment that you'll be painted as some sort of noble victim. You're an attractive young woman who had an affair with a married father of four. You're a homewrecker, who's thrown all her toys out of the pram when things didn't go her way –

LEONA: /I am not a homewrecker!

KATHRYN: Aren't you? You're a good person Leona – I know that. You're intelligent, kind and you work bloody hard – but that's not how you'll be depicted. You did have an affair. They'll tear you apart – every past relationship, every message you and he sent to each other, every last detail of your sexual activities.... Just take a moment and think about it, after hearing all of that, are the public going to see you as the decent person you really are, or are they going to see a publicity hungry trouble maker?

LEONA: Well I'm willing to take that risk for the sake of justice.

KATHRYN: Justice ... justice is a wonderful thing. Righting wrongs, standing up for the vulnerable, empowering the weak. It's what I've always fought for and it's what I will continue to fight for. Which is why I do want justice now.

Kathryn moves the orchids to the centre of the desk, side by side, a little distance apart.

Every time an unjust act is committed the world loses a little bit of its beauty ... things seem more bleak....

She tentatively pulls one petal from one of the flowers whilst delivering the following.

Woman who has only ever tried to help people, etc. gets callously raped by a vengeful ex-lover. Injustice.

She goes to the second flower, pulls off a petal.

Khotso Khongoana forced into marriage gets raped by her legally polygamous husband, contracts hiv and is ostracised by her entire community.... Injustice.

Kathryn continues to pull petals from the second flower, each time she does she lists another horrific abuse that some of the girls that they have been working with have been subject to.

Seso, Atile and Nyakallo, just a few of the young girls in Lesotho who are conditioned to believe that habitual beatings by their husbands, brothers and fathers is a legitimate form of displaying affection ... injustice. Ada Balewa, a child of ten, is sold to a man who believes that sexual intercourse with a virgin will cure him of aids ... injustice. Seinoli Ramoshabe erroneously detained in police custody for questioning in Maseru has her hands and knees bound together for 24 hours while she is sexually assaulted with a wooden club ... injustice. Injustice injustice injustice Injustice injustice injustice Injustice injustice injustice.

She continues until the second flower is completely decimated. Then, whilst motioning to the two flowers – one still almost entirely intact, the other completely destroyed. –

How's your justice looking now?

Leona, visibly shaken and thrown by Kathryn 's violent and provocative outburst, picks up her fallen petal, softly rubs it between her fingers and holds it to her chest.

Ends.

Afterword

Gabrielle Curtis and Clare Joy Langford

With *The Petal and The Orchid*, we wanted to write a piece that portrays two complex female characters faced with an impossible dilemma. We were particularly compelled by the idea of relationship rape as a theme, as this is something which remains an issue for women (and men) today, but is often not given validity, even by those involved. As the issue has grown in prominence in recent years and months, we felt that now was an apt time to excavate it. We sought to create a piece driven by conflict, where there really is no straightforward course of action. Context and high stakes were crucial, hence the setting of a charity dealing with female victims of horrific sexual abuse in the developing world. We spent a lot of time researching this area in order to get to the real heart of the conflict. The detail of the abuses needed to be shocking, accurate and explicit. Thus it becomes a case of "sex crime" vs. "sex crime", and the inevitable but uncomfortable "hierarchising of rape" that Kathryn describes, catapulting the piece into the realm of moral relativism. With Kathryn, it's hard to imagine any other situation in which she, a self-proclaimed defender of women's rights, would react in the way that she does when a female junior colleague reaches out for help. With Leona, we sought to explore how an otherwise virtuous woman could suddenly be faced with a depiction of herself as a villain because of uniquely cruel circumstances. Both women have a journey, in which they are forced to fight against their instincts and confront difficult realities, subverting audience expectations in the process.

11 *Copycat*

Tatty Hennessy

Characters

BRYONY, *late twenties, dressed to 'party'!*
GEM, *late twenties, more 'conservative' appearance than Bryony.*

Notes

(–) at the end of a line indicates being cut off.
(…) indicates where speech trails off.
(/) indicates the point where the immediately following dialogue interrupts.
(Beat) indicates a brief break in the dialogue.
(Pause) indicates where there is a thought process happening.

Original production details

Copycat was commissioned and produced by Little Pieces of Gold at Southwark Playhouse on 18 June 2017.

The cast was as follows:

BRYONY	Louisa Hollway
GEM	Sarah Kate Howard
Director:	Christopher Adams

Late night/early morning in Bryony's living room. Gem helps a very inebriated Bryony into her flat. Bryony is dressed for a night out. Gem is too, though more conservatively.

GEM: Here you go.
BRYONY: Oh my God you're a star I am so sorry.
GEM: That's alright babe, it happens.
BRYONY: No this is so fucking embarrassing, I cannot believe it. Oh god.
GEM: Got your water, go on, sit.

Gem helps Bryony onto the sofa.

BRYONY: Fuck. How much was the uber?

GEM: Don't worry.

BRYONY: I gotta pay you.

GEM: It's alright, I'm not far.

BRYONY: Oh, Jesus. Fuck. You're so nice. Thank you.

GEM: S'aright.

BRYONY: I am such a state.

GEM: Nice place. One bed, is it?

BRYONY: It's a fucking mess I wasn't…. Woss your name again babe?

GEM: Gem.

BRYONY: Thank you so much for helping me.

GEM: That's alright.

BRYONY: My friends just disappeared, I couldn't –

GEM: Happens to all of us.

BRYONY: Fuckers.

GEM: You lost sight of 'em, that's all.

BRYONY: I think they went to the bar, or I went to the bar.

GEM: You were outside, babe.

BRYONY: That's it. Some man by the bar kept grabbing at me and I had to get out
    and if Harry'd been there he'd have decked him but I was all on my own.

GEM: Here, have some water.

BRYONY: Ohh god.

GEM: Everything spinning? (Bryony nods) You gonna puke?

Bryony shakes her head and holds her hand over her mouth.

BRYONY: This is so embarrassing.

GEM: Don't be silly.

BRYONY: Never normally drink this much.

GEM: We all do it. Got to let loose sometime, haven't you? You live alone?

BRYONY: Flatmate. Sarah. She's on holiday. He's such a dick.

GEM: Who?

BRYONY: Harry.

GEM: That's his name, your boyfriend?

Bryony nods, fighting tears. Gem rubs Bryony's shoulders.

GEM: It's alright.

BRYONY: Why do we fucking bother?

GEM: Cos we love 'em.

BRYONY: Yeah. I just. Sometimes I don't think he loves me very much.

GEM: Their brains are built different to ours, that's all. They show it different.
    You gotta like, decode it, you know? They can't just be straight about it cos

they don't know how so they wrap it all up in other stuff and you gotta like, translate it.

BRYONY: Yeah?

GEM: Yeah. They're not like us.

BRYONY: No.

GEM: Apparently it's cos In the old days men would go out hunting by themselves and all the women would stay together in the caves with the children so the men didn't ever really need to talk that much.

BRYONY: Really?

GEM: Yeah. Makes sense if you think about it. You alright, feeling dizzy?

BRYONY: No, I'm alright.

GEM: Go on, have a bit more. That's it. (The bottle. Bryony drinks. Gem jokily pokes her ribs and puts on a 'lad' voice.) Get it down ya! Waaay.

BRYONY: (Laughs, feebly) Thanks. God, you're nice.

GEM: Nah.

BRYONY: You are. I wish everyone was as nice as drunk girls are to other drunk girls they've never met in toilets.

GEM: Be exhausting! Can you imagine? (Puts on a voice) Babe, I love your earrings.

BRYONY: (Joins in) That colour is so good on you, babes, you are rocking it, seriously.

GEM: (Continues) He's not worth it, babe, he's not worth it.

They both laugh.

BRYONY: Maybe you're right. God I'm gonna feel shit in the morning.

GEM: Yeah.

BRYONY: You think I should forgive him them? What he done?

GEM: Dunno. D'you love him?

BRYONY: I think so. Yeah.

GEM: Well. I think if you love someone you gotta do all you can to keep them, haven't you?

BRYONY: Maybe.

GEM: That's what I think. (Beat) And I think it's hard for them, sometimes. They're not like us.

Beat.

BRYONY: You got a boyfriend?

GEM: Yeah.

BRYONY: That's nice. What's he like?

GEM: He's alright, yeah. One of the good ones.

BRYONY: You love him?

GEM: (Smiles almost sadly) Yeah.

BRYONY: That's nice. (Holds her head) I feel funny.

GEM: Here (the water). You were pretty wasted.

BRYONY: Dizzy, like … Thank god you were there, babe, I'd be in the fucking gutter. Were you out with him tonight, your fella?

GEM: No.

BRYONY: Girls' night.

GEM: Yeah. (Pause) He's banged up actually. My boyfriend.

BRYONY: Shit.

GEM: Yeah.

BRYONY: I'm am so sorry. Jesus.

GEM: Yeah. He didn't do it, though. What they said he's done.

BRYONY: Of course he didn't. Oh, babe, I'm so sorry.

GEM: Drink your water.

BRYONY: You miss him?

GEM: Yeah. It's weird what you miss. I always used to wake up before him cos he liked a lie-in and I'd just stay in bed and stare at him and I miss that. I miss the hair in his ears.

BRYONY: You really do love him, then. I'm always on at Harry to do something about the state of his ears. Like an old man.

Gem smiles.

GEM: D'you ever get, like…. Sometimes I've got so much love inside me for him I feel like I've drunk acid. And it's trying to burn its way out of me. D'you ever feel that?

Gem looks at Bryony.

BRYONY: Yeah. Yeah, some of the time.

GEM: D'you think blokes feel that for us?

Beat.

BRYONY: I'm sure some of them do.

GEM: Drink your water.

BRYONY: How long's he away for?

GEM: 25 years. Finish it.

BRYONY: That's a long time.

GEM: Yeah. But I'm getting him out.

BRYONY: You got a lawyer?

GEM: Something like that. Is it finished?

BRYONY: I/feel a bit.

Gem holds the bottle to Bryony's mouth to stop her talking. Helps Bryony drink, almost forcibly.

GEM: I watched this documentary. On Netflix. American guy got done for murder. They said he killed this bloke and took out his organs and wrote all this like, cult stuff on the walls in his blood, right? But then after he was in prison all these other blokes were murdered in exactly the same way, blood on the walls, everything. So they knew they had the wrong guy, you see, cos the killer was still out there. And they let him go.

BRYONY: They said your bloke's in a cult?

GEM: (Laughs) No, they just say he killed a girl he met in a club. (Beat) Put something in her drink, took her home. Tried to shag her. And killed her. Apparently. But he wouldn't, you see. Cos he loves me.

Bryony looks at the empty water bottle.

BRYONY: (Heavily slurred, barely conscious) You.

Gem takes a small knife out of her handbag.

BRYONY: No.

A scuffle, but Bryony is drowsy now and Gem overpowers her, pinning her, maybe pulling her hair to keep her head still.

GEM: Please don't make it difficult. I'm really sorry. It's nothing to do with you. I quite like you, actually. It's just. He didn't do it. I know he didn't. Because he loves me. And I love him. And when you love someone, you do everything you can. You understand.

Gem stabs Bryony in the stomach. She stands, shaking. She wipes the knife. Bryony whimpers. Gem looks around.

GEM: It's a nice place, this.

Ends.

Afterword

Tatty Hennessy

I wrote this short back in December 2016. Trump had just won the election, the Women's March was fomenting and every woman I knew seemed to be running on rage. The revelation that so many (white) women had voted for Trump in that election surprised a lot of people, but to me this internalisation of misogyny and reinforcement of the patriarchy by women was as saddening as it was familiar. I wanted to write a play that explored this phenomenon. I wanted to look at how a society that allows vicious men to get away with bad behaviour while scrutinising and penalising women for slight transgressions, pits women against each other in an endless war for the finite commodity of men's affections, and vilifies and trivialises female rites of friendship, doesn't only harm women but pushes them to harm themselves, believing that harm to be self-preservation.

12 *Girlboss*

Corinne Salisbury

Characters

HAYLEY, *early twenties.*
ARTHUR, *early twenties.*
SINEAD, *late thirties.*

Notes

(/) marks the point where the immediately following dialogue interrupts.
(–) at the end of a line indicates being cut off.
(…) at the end of a speech or line means it trails off. On its own it indicates a pressure or expectation to speak.
(Beat) indicates a brief break in the dialogue.
(Pause) indicates where there is a thought process happening.

Original production details

Girlboss was commissioned and produced by Little Pieces Gold at Southwark Playhouse on 18 June 2017.

The cast was as follows:

HAYLEY	Amy Bowden
ARTHUR	Aaron Douglas
SINEAD	Kate Russell Smith
Director:	Georgie Staight

An anonymous corporate meeting room. Sinead and Arthur sit. Hayley, having just entered, stands looking at them.

HAYLEY: (With emphasis) Wow.
SINEAD: Sit down please, Hayley.
HAYLEY: What am I looking at here?!
SINEAD: I'm sorry, I was sure you received the emails?

HAYLEY: Um, you know I did.

SINEAD: So you know this is a disciplinary. (Beat) I'm sorry we have to use that word – it's so, hard, I know. But we have to be clear.

HAYLEY: Yes thanks Sinead I knew there was some kinda complaint, but Jesus … this guy??

ARTHUR: This is what I'm talking about Sinead, I I/can't –

SINEAD: I know. Just take a breath.

HAYLEY: Seriously? Is this a joke?

SINEAD: Please sit down.

Beat. Hayley takes her time slightly rearranging the position of her chair. She sits.

SINEAD: Arthur has made some quite serious complaints about you, Hayley.

HAYLEY: Uh huh.

SINEAD: So this meeting is to discuss his allegations in as fair and balanced a way as –

HAYLEY: Is he okay? He's shaking. Are you shaking Arthur?

ARTHUR: No –

HAYLEY: I'm just concerned with his wellbeing. That's the word of the moment isn't it?

SINEAD: I certainly think so.

HAYLEY: You're all over the wellbeing aren't you Sinead. Remember you had to spend the whole of the Christmas party in the loos, didn't you, holding Laura's hair while she vomited up all that mulled wine. Nearly got it on my shoes. Must have to deal with a lot of mess.

ARTHUR: She didn't have to.

HAYLEY: Pardon me, I didn't hear that Arthur?

SINEAD: I'm sorry if this is difficult for you Hayley.

HAYLEY: Why are you sorry? It's not your fault. Why should you be sorry?

Beat.

SINEAD: It's a figure of speech.

Hayley gives a contemptuous little shrug. Beat.

SINEAD: So. How this works is that I give a run-down of each of Arthur's griev-
ances. Then I give you the opportunity to respond to them all. Then Arthur has the chance to respond to your responses. And hopefully that opens up a dialogue which leads to a resolution.

HAYLEY: What's a resolution?

ARTHUR: (Quietly) I can get you a dictionary….

HAYLEY: Don't patronise me Arthur –

SINEAD: Let's all take a breath. Okay?

HAYLEY: What do you mean by resolution? What sort of thing are you after?

SINEAD: Ideally, an agreement on both sides to address the grievance and work together to prevent any future, disharmony.

HAYLEY: And if not?

SINEAD: Well, then I do a report, pass it to senior management and they decide on further processes to implement, possibly mediation, changing how you communicate, etcetera. Don't worry, you're not getting fired! Or I mean, that's not an option on the table at this point at all. And I want this to be an open dialogue today, so feel free to say whatever you need to say. I'm not recording you! I just tick some boxes on a form at the end, evaluate how successful this was.

HAYLEY: That's it.

SINEAD: That's the rules. I just do what I'm told. (Beat) Is that okay?

HAYLEY: Why do you ask – I don't have any say in it do I.

Sinead breathes and smiles.

SINEAD: Does anyone need anything? You warm enough? Hot drink? Arthur you're a tea man aren't you? Hayley I only ever see you drinking those impressive protein smoothies....

HAYLEY: I'm fine.

ARTHUR: I'm fine.

SINEAD: So – like I said I'll outline Arthur's complaints one by one –

HAYLEY: Why doesn't he outline them?

ARTHUR: That's not how it's done, Hayley.

HAYLEY: Oh that's not how it's done.

SINEAD: Someone from HR communicates the grievances. So that it doesn't feel like an attack – because it's coming from someone neutral, not from the complainant themselves.

HAYLEY: Neutral. Right.

SINEAD: Okay. So. I'm just going to read out a quick summary of each point, and would ask that you wait until I'm finished before you respond, please. Does that sound okay?

Hayley just stares at the pointlessness of the question. Sinead takes her time finding the relevant bit of paper.

SINEAD: Well. Point one is about the use of language to demean Arthur and undermine his confidence. I should say language includes body language. (Hayley suppresses a smile) For instance, on the 12th of October you said his rapport with clients was non-existent and no-one would buy ad space off a posh, stuttering bargain-bin Cumberbatch. On the 5th of December you interrupted him in a strategy meeting six times, and sighed and shook your head every time he spoke.

HAYLEY: (Quietly) Aw, diddums.

SINEAD: (Slightly louder) On the 22nd of February you responded to his advice about how you might edit your sales spreadsheets by suggesting he edit how much of a fuckwit he is.

HAYLEY: That was …
ARTHUR: You don't get to …
HAYLEY: That was meant to motivate!
SINEAD: Please, if you don't mind Hayley. Point two is about social exclusion. On at least four occasions he overheard you talking about him in negative terms to colleagues, and says that you frequently discourage colleagues from inviting him on work nights out.

Hayley suppresses a laugh.

SINEAD: Point three, lack of trust. You double-check his workings and send him constant reminders of every task on his list. You email his clients to ask if they're happy with his work. You repeatedly send him links to courses for confidence-building and social skills.
HAYLEY: I'm trying to help. I'm trying to help!

Pause. She takes in their stares.

HAYLEY: That is a lot of detail, Arthur. That is a lot of dates and statistics.
ARTHUR: I tried to talk to you directly. I never wanted it to come to this.
HAYLEY: Did you log them? All these incidents? Did you write every insult in your diary at night? Maybe you found it therapeutic. Cathartic?
ARTHUR: (Muttering) Not even half of it.
HAYLEY: Pardon?
ARTHUR: There's loads more. That's just … (Quietly) You keep nicking my lunch.

Hayley tries again to suppress a laugh. Fails.

HAYLEY: I do not.
ARTHUR: Green tupperware, that's mine.
HAYLEY: Of course, only you would cook a week's worth of turd-coloured lentil stew and bring it in in tubs labelled for each day.
ARTHUR: You see/she's –
HAYLEY: Oh, Jeez, your life must be so hard –
SINEAD: Please, both, this isn't helpful. Hayley what you need to do now is –
HAYLEY: Respond. I know. Respond to … this. (Beat) Why is it only Arthur?
SINEAD: What do you mean?
HAYLEY: I know I've rubbed a few other people up the wrong way. You must've heard a bit.
SINEAD: I can't refer to any informal chatter in this meeting, this is only about Arthur's grievance.
HAYLEY: But you've heard. (Beat) So why is Arthur the only one that's gone through the formal channels? I'll tell you, shall I? Because he's the Only Man in the team. They brought us all on at the same time, and yeah we're

competing against each other, yeah we have targets, not everyone is going to make the cut. So sure I throw my weight around a bit, I'm not afraid to speak up when I disagree with someone. Why should I be? Why should I apologise for that? I'm pushing my co-workers to see who's the strongest – to make them stronger. And we'll end up with a final team that's more efficient, more resilient as a result. But guess who's the only one to find this situation utterly intolerable? Oh right, the man. Because women can handle a shit ton more than men can. Women just fucking get on with it. Whereas this one – red trouser brigade here – who's never had a taste of adversity his whole life … Of course he's the one to go all hysterical.

Pause.

ARTHUR: (Quietly) From hystera. Greek for womb.
HAYLEY: What?
ARTHUR: Men can't actually get hysterical. Technically.
HAYLEY: Oh that's what you think is it, princess –
SINEAD: Hayley. It seems –
HAYLEY: And besides, so many times he needed shouting down, he needed a reality check. He doesn't know what he's talking about most of the time.
ARTHUR: That is a baseless accusation.
HAYLEY: We do advertising tie-ins for a beauty magazine, Sinead! He doesn't have the expertise. How could he?
ARTHUR: I have a Masters in Strategic Marketing.
HAYLEY: You see how condescending he is? So many times I've seen him just bellow his opinions, shoehorn them in when they're not needed, when no-one asked him, and he gives off this air of expertise that is based on nothing, and I'm supposed to not challenge that? But you wouldn't know that. You don't know. HR. You're separate. You're neutral. You're not in the room, you don't see how things really go down. You only have his word for it.

Beat.

SINEAD: He doesn't bellow. He speaks at a normal volume.
HAYLEY: How do you know?
SINEAD: And he doesn't actually give his opinion that often. His method is to observe, listen and learn, wait and then make a considered proposal. Would that be fair to say Arthur?
HAYLEY: That's what he's told you?
SINEAD: No. I've had several members of your team independently tell me this.

Beat.

HAYLEY: You asked them.
SINEAD: It's come up naturally. When we chat.

HAYLEY: Thought you weren't meant to bring gossip and rumour into this meeting.

SINEAD: This isn't gossip. It's a pretty clear picture. (Beat) See the thing is Hayley, just to explain, if I can – because I'm neutral, I don't take sides. People trust me. People confide in me. It's easy for me to get a sense of what's going on. I don't need to go about investigating. You imagine me, hanging around in a deerstalker, binoculars? People come to me.

ARTHUR: So she knows you're lying, Hayley.

SINEAD: I'm sorry but that's too strong a word, Arthur. (Beat) Are you sure you don't want a glass of water Hayley?

HAYLEY: I was fat as a teenager. I was fucking fat. (Beat) You have any idea what it's like being a fat teenage girl? Coming from where I come from? How hard it is to get people to not see you as target or doormat? I know what it looks like when a man doesn't think I'm worth the air I'm breathing. I can tell. I can always tell. I've lived with it for long enough. You can't see it Sinead because you haven't lived it. But I swear to god, it's real.

Pause.

SINEAD: Must have been really hard.

HAYLEY: Yeah well.

SINEAD: Did your friends defend you?

HAYLEY: They – sometimes.

SINEAD: I hope you had people on your side. Who loved you unconditionally. We all need that.

HAYLEY: Of course I did. Why wouldn't I?

SINEAD: What made you start to get in shape? Was it something someone said?

HAYLEY: Something like that.

SINEAD: He must have been a real dick. Excuse my language.

HAYLEY: He was.

They smile at each other slightly.

But cruelty motivates, Sinead. That's what I'm saying. Cruelty motivates.

SINEAD: You close with your family?

HAYLEY: Why?

SINEAD: You never talk about them. Everyone needs a support network.

HAYLEY: I'm not everyone.

SINEAD: That's certainly true. I think that's one thing we can all agree on.

HAYLEY: What does that mean?

SINEAD: You're so driven. And you're fearless. Those are such rare qualities in a new recruit, especially if you don't mind me saying a female one. I'm not surprised you stood out. What happened, in the past, with bullying or … well, this might sound mad and I might just be being a daft old thing, but a little bit of me almost wants to thank them. For making you this fearless person. This person with so, so much potential – the air practically vibrates with it.

HAYLEY: Well.

SINEAD: (Smiling) It begins with a T H....

HAYLEY: Thanks.

SINEAD: I wonder Hayley if you get a bit combative, if it's a bit of a reflex, to tar all men with the same brush, so to speak, treat them all as a potential threat? Almost like you imagine them disrespecting you with everything they say and do – every time they tell you anything it's mansplaining, every time they offer help it's patronising? Which is understandable. Given your past experiences. But not, totally, fair, I would venture to say?

Pause. Hayley looks from Sinead to Arthur and back again.

HAYLEY: (Slowly) I don't think.... It's not ... that simple....

SINEAD: I'm getting the sense that you're receptive to this idea Hayley?

Beat. Hayley doesn't look at them.

ARTHUR: It's a miracle.

HAYLEY: What?

SINEAD: Arthur.

HAYLEY: Don't you fucking dare, you don't know what I'm thinking, you don't know what's going on up here.

ARTHUR: Just a whole lot of rage and tumbleweed, it's always seemed to me.

SINEAD: Calm down.

ARTHUR: What after how she's treated me, I'm not allowed to hit back?

HAYLEY: That was you hitting back was it? Ouch.

ARTHUR: You have any idea what you do to people? Some days I can't face getting up in the morning.

HAYLEY: Well I'm sure your Mum makes you alphabetti spaghetti and you feel much better.

ARTHUR: It takes some serious insecurity to go through life seeing every inter-action as a fight you've gotta win.

HAYLEY: When you're a woman, in this business, it is. And if I was a man no-one would blink at my behaviour. So you think I'm gonna apologise for wanting to get ahead? For trying to be successful? I am never apologising for that.

ARTHUR: Do you listen to yourself ever?

HAYLEY: Oh fuck you, you fucking crybaby.

SINEAD: Hayley, I will not have that language in this room.

HAYLEY: What cos you don't like it, cos it's not nice?

SINEAD: Yes. That's exactly it. It's not nice. And niceness, Hayley – niceness is a more powerful force than you seem able to understand. You seem to think that because I'm kind I'm also weak. But it is not weakness to have time for everyone. To try and understand everyone – to show interest. Even in a little budding psychopath like you. I have tried, I really have, because I always try – that is the principle I live my life by. But I've had enough. It may not have occurred to you Hayley, but you're not the only one in this room who calls themselves a feminist. Except when I use the word, it's not as an improvised excuse for lazy cruelty. I have had enough of this argument that men are inherently cruel, it's a man's world, so to get ahead we have to play by their rules and not show an ounce of shame whoever we hurt. "Sorry" considered the worst expletive of all! When did "being a dick" get rebranded as empowerment? Niceness isn't weakness, Hayley. It's strength. And you know what else is strength? Being adult enough to acknowledge your mistakes. You know who doesn't do that? A child. So can I invite you to take some fucking responsibility. Please?

Pause. Hayley, stunned, recovers. Smiles.

HAYLEY: Now we're cooking.

Sinead looks away, breathes.

HAYLEY: Why don't you take some responsibility, Sinead? You say you're just following the rules, you have no say in this process blah blah. But you could make a decision about what should happen to me, couldn't you? If you're so strong.

Pause.

SINEAD: I plan to, Hayley. I do make the decision about what happens next. I suggested otherwise at the start, because I knew you would speak more freely. Which gives me much more to go on.

HAYLEY: Right. Well. That wasn't very nice.

SINEAD: So what should I write in my report, do you think? I could leave out the worst of what's been said here today – but include some contextualising detail about your past, campaign for better understanding of the roots of your behaviour – I could suggest the two of you have learnt to understand each other better, and you Hayley have made a commitment to change your attitude. After you apologised, of course. (Beat) Because if I report what's really been said today, dismissal would be pretty inevitable I'm afraid.

HAYLEY: That's not fair – I thought this was....

SINEAD: You thought I was safe? I could write a report that would give you a second chance, Hayley. I could give you the benefit of the doubt. I could move Arthur to another department so neither of you would have to encounter the other. That would be being nice, wouldn't it? (Beat) But you would owe me. Wouldn't you?

Beat.

HAYLEY: What would you want?

SINEAD: Niceness, of course. That's what I'd want in return. (Beat) We could start now. We could have a little practice run.

HAYLEY: Involving what?

SINEAD: Well. (She thinks) Why don't you look at Arthur now and tell him three things you like about him? And name an instance when you benefited from his help. Is that okay with you, Arthur?

ARTHUR: Yeah, I reckon I can handle that.

Hayley is stood, in Fight or Flight pose. She looks at them both. They wait.

Ends.

Afterword

Corinne Salisbury

This play was born out of a particular frustration, which boiled over when I watched the first episode of a certain new Netflix series of the same name. As a card-carrying feminist, I was nonetheless growing extremely weary of seeing feminism used to justify celebrating the actions and behaviour of every female ever, regardless of what these actions involve, regardless of how cruel, thoughtless, self-centred or destructively capitalist. Assertiveness as a guaranteed virtue in its own right, no matter to what end. Kindness, humility, generosity and self-awareness seen as weaknesses to be stamped out. So this play was an attempt to vent some of these feelings. I hoped it would spark off some thoughts in the audience, one way or another.

Part V

To connect or dis-connect?

13 *Swipe*

Grace Ivana Carroll

Characters

FELICITY, *22, perfectly made-up and put together.*
ANNA, *21, fresh faced and a little scruffy.*

Notes

(/) marks the point where the immediately following dialogue interrupts.
(…) at the end of a speech means it trails off. On its own it indicates a pressure or expectation to speak.
(Beat) indicates a brief break in the dialogue.

Original production details

Swipe was commissioned and produced by Little Pieces of Gold at Southwark Playhouse on 4 February 2018.

The cast was as follows:

FELICITY	Hayley Osborne
ANNA	Evelyn Lockley
Director:	Jodie E. Burgess

Scene One

Felicity and Anna sit at a table together in a café. They are both engrossed in their phones and swiping on Tinder.

ANNA: This is fun.
FELICITY: Hmm.
ANNA: Such a great idea. It's so simple.

Felicity carries on swiping.

ANNA: You're right. I should have downloaded this ages ago.

They continue swiping.

ANNA: Oh this one is tricky. I can't decide. Look at him for me.
FELICITY: No way I'm on a roll. My goal is to get ten matches in the next five minutes.
ANNA: I don't know. From his pictures he seems like he could either be super interesting or a massive dick.
FELICITY: What's his bio?
ANNA: Just says he's a project manager. Oh wait, there's more.

Beat.

ANNA: "I'm a free spirited old-fashioned Bohemian soul in a new age skin, and a freethinking philosophical poet."

Felicity stops swiping. Long beat where they just stare at each other incredulously.

FELICITY: Where does it say he works?
ANNA: Barclays.

Beat.

FELICITY: No.

Anna swipes left. They carry on swiping.

ANNA: Why would you write that?
FELICITY: The confidence of men continues to astound me.
ANNA: Oh someone has super liked me!

Beat.

ANNA: What's that?
FELICITY: It's like swiping right but you can only use it once a day.
ANNA: Oh that's cool right?
FELICITY: Not really it's consistently used by those annoying type of guys, who's like your co-worker or on your course or something, some activity where you're forced to be together and he's always overly nice to you even though you've shown no interest in him, and then random people come up to you and are like "Oh Steve really likes you, you guys would be so cute together" and you're like "I don't really know Steve" and they're like "Just give him a chance" and you're like "I don't want to" and then they look at you like you're a bitch and then you have no friends and it's all because you wouldn't fuck some random guy called Steve.

Anna looks at her.

ANNA: Personal experience of that?
FELICITY: Super likes are emotional blackmail, don't buy into it.
ANNA: I already swiped right.
FELICITY: Anna!
ANNA: It was too mean to go left!
FELICITY: You have to be more ruthless.
ANNA: Oh he's already messaged.
FELICITY: Of course he has! You're probably way out of his league.
ANNA: He said "Hey! How are you today? Hope your day is going great."
    Exclamation point, smiley face.
FELICITY: Oh lord.

Anna's phone DINGS.

ANNA: It's him again. He says, "Just to say you have very beautiful eyes" then a
    smiley face with tongue sticking out.
FELICITY: He's going to chop you up into tiny pieces.
ANNA: He's just being nice.

DING.

ANNA: "and very lovely kissable lips."
FELICITY: Ew.
ANNA: Yeah that was a bit much.

DING.

ANNA: Oh god him again. "How's your day going" and then three question marks.
FELICITY: That's what you get with a super like.

DING.

ANNA: Oh someone else messaged me.

Beat.

ANNA: "Wanna sit on my face?" Ewww.
FELICITY: Yeah before I got this app I didn't realise how many guys wanted me
    to sit on their faces.
ANNA: Another one. "Just to let you know I don't want anything serious." That's
    nice he's being honest.

Felicity rolls her eyes.

DING.

ANNA: "But I promise you will have a good time, I make all the ladies squirt lol." Oh god what is this?

FELICITY: I wish every time a guy promised I'd have a good time, he could sign a legally binging contract where he'd be forced to give me some sort of compensation if I didn't orgasm.

ANNA: So is this what dating is now? Fending off messages from sexually aggressive men and the occasional nice but creepy guy?

FELICITY: Isn't that always what dating has been?

ANNA: Okay I think I might be done.

Anna puts her phone down. Felicity looks up.

FELICITY: What?

ANNA: Tinder. It's not for me.

FELICITY: Oh come on. You've been on it for all of five minutes.

ANNA: The guys on it are too sleazy.

FELICITY: It's not that men on it are too sleazy. It's that men are sleazy.

ANNA: That can't be true.

FELICITY: Trust me it is. They can just be more open about it in these apps.

ANNA: None of the guys I know are sleazy.

FELICITY: Not to your face. It's like how every guy you meet swears he has never sent a dick pic. Yet every girl you know has been sent one.

ANNA: That doesn't mean.... You're generalising.

FELICITY: Tinder isn't a gross place. The world is a gross place and Tinder is just being honest about it. That's what I like. It gets to the point. Left or right, yes or no. Guys are either sleazebags or semi decent.

ANNA: But there's something weirdly impersonal about swiping on faces. It feels like a game.

FELICITY: Sweetie, life's a game.

ANNA: Why can't I just meet someone naturally?

FELICITY: And how would you do that?

ANNA: I don't know. (Starts to daydream) Maybe I'm taking a walk and I'm carrying some books or something, and then I drop one.

FELICITY: Books? Plural?

ANNA: Yeah ... and then he picks one up and he's like/

FELICITY: Why are you carrying multiple books?

ANNA: I don't know, maybe I'm moving? Stop interrupting! And then he helps me pick them up and he sees a book and says "oh my god that's totally my favourite book" and then we start talking and it just like ... happens.

Anna looks dreamy eyed. Felicity stares at her in disbelief.

FELICITY: You want to live in a Jane Austen Novel?

ANNA: At least there's romance in a Jane Austen Novel.

FELICITY: Romance is a myth. You want to live in a time where men were picked out for you?

ANNA: Maybe.

FELICITY: Anna!

ANNA: What? I'm terrible at dating.

FELICITY: You're asking for the choice to be taken away. Women have fought for the right to choose and you're just throwing it away.

ANNA: The right to receive anonymous sleazy messages?

FELICITY: No the right to choose your own partner, your own destiny! We now have endless men to choose from, and they're all right in our pocket.

ANNA: I guess.

Anna sulks.

Anna's phone DINGS. She looks at it for a second. She smiles. She starts to type. Felicity looks at her suspiciously.

FELICITY: What are you doing?

ANNA: Just texting a friend.

Anna's phone DINGS again.

FELICITY: Texts don't make that noise. You're messaging someone on the App! I thought you said you wanted someone from the olden times.

ANNA: This one seems nice! He said Breaking Bad is also his favourite show and he also is a big fan of cheddar cheese.

Felicity looks confused.

ANNA: I said in my bio those were my favourite things.

Anna looks at the message and smiles again.

ANNA: Oh my god he's so funny.

FELICITY: Babe try not to get too excited. You have to talk to other people. Play it cool.

ANNA: (Not really listening) Yeah, yeah sure.

Anna's on her phone again.

ANNA: Maybe this isn't so bad.

FELICITY: I told you.

ANNA: Ah he seems sweet. I just went on his profile and it says he's an oceanologist. That's really cool.

FELICITY: That is cool.

ANNA: Maybe he could get us free tickets for the Aquarium.

Anna giggles.

FELICITY: What?

ANNA: Just thinking how cool it would be to say "This is my boyfriend Jamie, he's an oceanologist."

Scene Two

Felicity sits on the same table swiping. Anna enters in a huff.

FELICITY: Hey, how was your date with Jamie?

ANNA: I don't want to talk about it.

FELICITY: Okay.

ANNA: He stood me up! Like actual stood me up. I was all dressed up and everything and then the fucker texted me two hours before we had to meet saying he had a "work thing" then he had the audacity to ask me to send nudes. How ungracious is that?

FELICITY: Really ungracious.

ANNA: What kind of disaster does an oceanologist even have? Who needs to desperately study the sea some more?

FELICITY: Well what about other guys?

ANNA: What other guys?

FELICITY: You have been speaking to other guys?

ANNA: No.

FELICITY: Anna! You have to organise multiple dates. So this doesn't happen.

ANNA: No I'm sure this was just one time thing. It's such a dick move.

FELICITY: Happened to me four times last week.

ANNA: What? Four times? Oh babes.

FELICITY: No it's fine. I always schedule two dates every night anyway.

ANNA: Two dates? How does that work?

FELICITY: Usually one of them begs off, but then I have a backup.

ANNA: What if neither of them does?

FELICITY: Then I pick the one I like best and call off the other one.

ANNA: But don't you feel bad?

FELICITY: Do you really think Jamie the oceanologist is feeling bad right now?

ANNA: True. I don't think he even was an oceanologist. He seemed surprised that dolphins were mammals.

FELICITY: See! Dating is a brutal world. You have to be ruthless, and follow certain rules.

ANNA: What rules do you follow?

FELICITY: Well, first one is you never kiss on the first date. Never message first. If he doesn't text you the night of the date, checking you got home all right, he's not interested, don't text him. Let him pay for the first round of drinks, but after that you offer. If he insists that's fine, if he doesn't insist, he's probably not that into you.

ANNA: Christ that's a lot.

FELICITY: You pick it up after a while.

ANNA: So how many boys did you go on a date with last week?

FELICITY: Six.

ANNA: (Shocked) Six?

FELICITY: (Shrugging) Just for drinks.

ANNA: That makes my head hurt. So how many of those did you actually like?

FELICITY: Two were disasters. Three were okay. One was kind of nice.

ANNA: Tell me about the kind of nice one.

FELICITY: Well he was sweet, funny, quite smart and really really fit.

ANNA: Great! So when are you going to see him again?

FELICITY: Oh I'm not.

ANNA: Why?

FELICITY: Well he worked in like insurance or something, and I had a guy once be a real dick to me that worked in insurance, and also he's like 5 foot 9 and my ex boyfriend was that and I remember that being really annoying because I couldn't wear my five inch heels around him.

Anna stares at Felicity, dumbstruck.

ANNA: What?

FELICITY: Plus we didn't have that (Thinks for a minute) something.

ANNA: I'm confused. What's the end goal here?

FELICITY: To, you know, have a relationship.

ANNA: And this is how to do it?

FELICITY: Yeah.

ANNA: But that's nonsense, you dumping a great sounding guy because he doesn't have that "something" is as stupid as me wanting to meet a guy in real life by dropping books.

FELICITY: The books thing is definitely stupider.

ANNA: Is it? You've been at this for months and months, and no trace of anyone. Isn't looking for that "something" at a certain point just as dumb as wanting a fairy tale? What if this something you're looking for just doesn't exist?

FELICITY: Look you don't know anything about dating, so just back off.

ANNA: All I know is that you are going on multiple dates, keeping people at arm's length, playing these ridiculous games because you're afraid of actually getting close to someone.

FELICITY: Don't be that person.

ANNA: What person?

FELICITY: That best friend in a rom-com who tells me to let my guard down and open myself up. It's passé and you're better than that. Plus I don't have to settle. I have options and so what if I want to explore them?

ANNA: Okay, fine, you do that then.

They sit in silence for a few seconds. Anna sips her coffee.

FELICITY: I'm having fun. I'm being young and single.

ANNA: I'm not saying anything.

FELICITY: Although, I am actually pretty tired of doing my contour make-up every night.

Anna nods thoughtfully.

FELICITY: Plus I would quite like to have a conversation with someone that isn't about how many brothers and sisters we both have and what kind of music we like.

Anna doesn't want to ruin this so she just listens.

FELICITY: Plus I have this real bad problem with my thumb where all it does is swipe now.

Felicity tries to bend her thumb and it just moves side to side.

FELICITY: Doctors say it may need surgery.

ANNA: Yikes.

FELICITY: Maybe I will just try another date with Tom.

ANNA: Is that his name?

FELICITY: Yeah. Maybe I don't feel much now, but something will grow.

ANNA: Exactly.

FELICITY: He was cute, kind of manly, but not laddy. He seems to really like me as well. He kept on like staring at me, and he's texted me so much today.

ANNA: I have a real good feeling about him.

Scene Three

Felicity is sitting by herself. She has her arms crossed and is really pissed off. Anna approaches with two coffee cups. She sets one down in front of Felicity.

ANNA: Vanilla Soy Latte! Your favourite!

Felicity keeps her arms crossed and avoids eye contact with Anna.

ANNA: Look I'm sorry. I don't know how many more times you want me to say it.

FELICITY: (Mimicking Anna in a silly voice) "Open yourself up Felicity, Give him a chance, let your guard down, he could surprise you." (Turns to Anna) You. That's what you sound like.

ANNA: I didn't know what he was going to turn out like.

FELICITY: I have my rules for a reason, to stop this precise thing from happening.

ANNA: Look I'm sorry it didn't turn out well but didn't it feel good to open yourself up to someone?

FELICITY: No.

ANNA: I guess that's the problem with having so many guys in our pockets. Guys have that many girls in their pockets as well.

FELICITY: Six other girls.

ANNA: So sleazy.

FELICITY: He didn't think it was serious so it was okay. Four months we'd been going out. I had been round to his family's house for Sunday dinner. I met his friends. I bought so much new underwear. I have so many ingrown hairs on my vagina now!

ANNA: How did he fit them all in?

FELICITY: One was only a Skype relationship and two girls he was apparently just sexting. That doesn't count apparently. (Sighs) I think I'm done.

ANNA: Done with what?

FELICITY: Dating.

ANNA: Seriously?

FELICITY: Yeah. You're right, maybe an arranged marriage would be a good thing. What's the modern version of that?

ANNA: That Married at First sight program?

FELICITY: Or Love Island?

ANNA: Please go on Love Island.

FELICITY: No all the men on there are too jacked. They look like croissants.

Anna's phone DINGS. She picks it up.

FELICITY: You still on it?

ANNA: Kind of. It's just someone asking if they can lick cheese off me. Since I put that cheese thing in my bio I get a lot of that.

FELICITY: Maybe we should get off dating apps.

ANNA: Then how would we meet anyone?

FELICITY: I don't know. How do other couples meet?

ANNA: Whenever I meet a couple they always say they met through friends.

FELICITY: (Grimacing) That would mean I would have to make friends.

ANNA: I don't want to make friends.

FELICITY: Every semi decent guy we know I shagged ages ago.

ANNA: I know right.

FELICITY: I hate those couples though that said they met "through friends".

ANNA: The girl's name is always Kate.

FELICITY: The guy's name is Chris.

ANNA: They met at uni. In Bath or Bristol.

FELICITY: They live in an attached house on the outskirts of the city.

ANNA: They live together for four years before getting engaged.

FELICITY: He works in tech. She works for a charity.

ANNA: They get engaged at 28.

FELICITY: They get married in Kent.

ANNA: They have a baby boy and name it something they think is alternative.

FELICITY: Not realising it's the most popular name in the country.

ANNA: Something like Noel or Jonah.

FELICITY: I mean imagine if our lives were like that.

ANNA: I would shoot myself in the head.

Beat.

ANNA: So if we don't want that, what do we want?

They stare at each other for a long beat.
Anna's phone DINGS. She picks it up.

ANNA: (Reading the message) "I'm going to whole foods, want me to pick you up anything?"

FELICITY: Good line.

ANNA: He stole it from Master of None.

FELICITY: Call him out on it. See how he reacts.

ANNA: I thought you were done with dating and apps?

FELICITY: I can be your dating adviser.

ANNA: My freelance dating consultant.

FELICITY: What's on his profile?

ANNA: (Looks) Ah a picture of him and his cat!

FELICITY: Let me see.

Afterword

Grace Ivana Carroll

I wanted to write *Swipe* because whenever I went to the theatre the women on stage didn't felt familiar to me. They didn't speak or act the way my friends and I do. Even when female characters were "great" they never felt real. I wanted to try and write female characters that I could know and be friends with. I wrote about dating apps because they were a big part of my life at the time. I was using them as were a lot of my friends, and we spent a lot of time debating their merits and disadvantages. I wanted to write about that rollercoaster of dating, of feeling overjoyed one minute and completely worthless the next. I wanted to explore whether dating apps had changed how people approached dating and whether having that many options was detrimental to finding a long-term romantic partner. I wanted to write about my friends and my own experiences, and find the humour in the pain that is modern dating.

Although the play is seemingly all about dating and boys, I'd like to think the heart of *Swipe* is about these two young women's friendship and how they bond over their dating fails. To me, it's a celebration of good friends; friends who are always by your side as you endure all the bad dates and failed relationships.

14 *Echoes Through the Dust*

Sarah Hehir

Characters

ZAMIRA, *early forties, Syrian.*
KATIE, *late teens, British (any ethnic background).*

Note

When Katie reads Zamira's blog posts, Zamira can join in at any time or even take over the narration entirely.

Original production details

Echoes Through The Dust was commissioned and produced by Little Pieces of Gold at Southwark Playhouse on 16 June 2014.

The cast was as follows:

ZAMIRA	Luisa Guerreiro
KATIE	Cassandra Bond
Director:	Madelaine Moore

The play is set during one night in a field hospital in Damascus and a maternity unit in Manchester in the winter of 2011. It is told through tweets and blog posts.

Zamira is a rebel fighter in the Free Syrian Army. She is the mother of a teenage girl and a young boy. Zamira and her husband have left their children in the care of a grandfather in order to fight against Assad's oppressive regime.

Katie is a young single mum in Wythenshawe Hospital – her baby has just been born and her Mum's train from Scotland is delayed.

Katie and Zamira are in hospital beds 2,000 miles apart.

KATIE: Compose new tweet: Katie @ Katie D
    Why did no fucker ever warn me about after-pains? They rock through my body like sick jokes

#deliveryunit Wythenshawe Hospital Manchester

ZAMIRA: Compose new tweet: Zamira @ rebel war

Damascus devastated. Bombs still falling. Maternity unit destroyed

war crimes

KATIE: The midwife tells me to sleep while the baby sleeps. I can't sleep. I can't even close my eyes.

ZAMIRA: Chaos outside. A constant stream of bodies are brought in.

A newborn baby's cries stir echoes through the dust.

Field hospital Damascus

KATIE: The midwife gives me a pain killer up my bum and I don't even care. I'll take anything

bring it on

ZAMIRA: The air is thick with pain. It's physical. There's nothing heroic about any of this.

KATIE: (Reads) 'National Rail Enquiries Alert. Glasgow Queen Street to Manchester Piccadilly. Delays at Falkirk until further notice.' Shit.

ZAMIRA: The baby is silent. A flurry of noise is followed by stillness. Slowly, his mother's broken cries choke the night with grief.

don't ignore Syria

KATIE: Text to Mum – where are you now? My alert on Twitter says Falkirk trains delayed. Are you caught up in it? Will you still get here by morning?

ZAMIRA: Wounded rebel soldiers stand beside old men bent double, beside orphans too tired to feel anything yet.

don't ignore Syria

KATIE: I stare out of the window at the lights of the city. The sun will come up eventually and no train is delayed forever. I pull the covers over my head and wait.

ZAMIRA: Medics battle against bacteria and short supplies. They shout to be heard above the shelling outside.

field hospital Damascus

KATIE: *SFX text alert.*

(Katie reads) Text from Mum. Still stuck at Falkirk. Hope to be moving soon. Sorry!

(Reads) Retweeted by Simon: Zamira @ rebel war

The baby is silent. A flurry of noise is followed by stillness. Slowly, his mother's broken cries choke the night with grief.

don't ignore Syria

Katie @ katie D

I look at my baby with her mad black hair sticking up. I touch her tiny arm and her hands fly out like she's scared of me. She stays asleep.

(Reads again) The baby is silent. A flurry of noise is followed by stillness. Slowly, his mother's broken cries choke the night with grief.

Tweet to Zamira @ rebel war

Why did the baby die?

ZAMIRA: Tweet to Katie @ Katie D

Bombs hit the maternity unit. His mother ran with him through the streets to find help. It was too late. He couldn't be saved.

KATIE: That's so sad. His poor Mum.

ZAMIRA: An army that targets civilians doesn't care who it kills. We need your support to win this war # free Syria
Please retweet.

KATIE: No I won't retweet. I won't use a baby's death to get you publicity. I don't even know who you are.

ZAMIRA: The baby that died here tonight, died because the regime wants to terrorise people. Fear shuts people up. Would you rather I kept quiet and said nothing?

KATIE: I don't know. It just feels wrong.
(Text to Mum) Do you remember what it was like when you had me? How did you feel in those first few hours? Which train are you on now? Are you heading for Preston yet?

Katie clicks on a link on Zamira's Twitter profile.

KATIE: (Reading) Zamira's blog. East of Damascus. One month ago. Snipers, hot sun, adrenalin. We run for cover: duck into a deserted house and wait, listening. We catch our breath as quietly as we can. I am so close to the soldier next to me that I can see sweat beading on the pores of her skin. Hijab askew and automatic rifle gripped, ready for use; she is the mirror image of me.
Follow Zamira @ rebel war

ZAMIRA: Thanks for the follow. Even though you don't agree with me.

KATIE: You're a soldier? You're actually fighting on the frontline?

ZAMIRA: Yes.

KATIE: I didn't know Muslim women fought in wars.

ZAMIRA: It's not so strange. Plenty of us do. pic.Twitter.com

KATIE: Which one is you?

ZAMIRA: The one in the middle, cleaning the weapons.

KATIE: You look like you're singing.

ZAMIRA: We're not always killing.

KATIE: You look fearless – in control.

ZAMIRA: It's easy to look brave when you're holding a gun.

KATIE: It's not only the army that kills ordinary people in Syria. You and your rebels do too!

ZAMIRA: By mistake maybe! The difference is, we're not targeting civilian populations!

KATIE: But they still die. Children too. I've seen. I've googled it. What makes what you're doing right?

ZAMIRA: If no-one rebels, we surrender to oppression. Maybe forever. People were murdered here for protesting peacefully. Google that.

KATIE: (Reading) Zamira's blog. East of Damascus. Two months ago. Damascus. The eastern suburb of Mhelia. Launching, dropping, firing, shelling.

This is how I speak now. I am learning a new language that snakes into my dreams like a foreign tongue. I clean my gun like a cooker, I prepare my weapons like dinner, killing is as commonplace as ringing the neck of a chicken. Almost. Mortars, rockets, barrel bombs. Casualties, martyrs, collateral damage. I am a rebel, an insurgent, a terrorist, a woman, an outrage, a disgrace. Brave. A western journalist takes photos of my face. I smile behind my veil as if for a family snapshot and I wonder how the world will see me.

Compose new tweet to: zamira @ rebel war

Are you helping out at the field hospital?

ZAMIRA: No. I've got a shard of shrapnel stuck in my skull. They won't let me leave until they've treated me.

KATIE: How bad is it?

ZAMIRA: The medic said a few millimetres to the left and I'd be dead.

KATIE: Fuck!

ZAMIRA: Not right now.

KATIE: Funny.

ZAMIRA: I'm going out of my mind in here.

KATIE: Me too. I feel exhausted and hyper at the same time. The nurse said I couldn't take anything to help me sleep in case I want to breastfeed.

ZAMIRA: You had a baby?

KATIE: Yeah. Just before midnight.

ZAMIRA: That's great! That's really great news!

KATIE: Thank you.

ZAMIRA: A boy or a girl?

KATIE: A girl. 5 lb 12 oz. With jet black hair.

ZAMIRA: How is she?

KATIE: They say she's doing fine. She looks ok. Just very tiny. I don't really know much about babies.

ZAMIRA: You'll learn quickly. How are you feeling?

KATIE: Ok.

ZAMIRA: Just ok?

KATIE: It all feels so new.

ZAMIRA: Is her Dad with you?

KATIE: Not anymore. He wanted to keep the baby. He persuaded me. Then he lost his job and lost the plot: said he wasn't ready to be a dad.

ZAMIRA: Oh. I'm sorry.

KATIE: I've been thinking that he might come back once he sees her. I think she looks a bit like him.

ZAMIRA: I'm sorry I bombarded you with civil war and tragedy. Not the right time.

KATIE: It's alright. Anyway, it was me who commented on your tweet.
(Reading) Zamira's blog East of Damascus three months ago. I see my husband for ten minutes. It feels like a painful opening of old wounds; a ripping of scar tissue. I don't cry when he holds me but I breathe in every-

thing: his salty skin, tobacco, musk and paraffin. He wipes his soldier's sleeve across his eyes to hide the tears. We sit on sandbags and smoke a cigarette. We drink mint tea. We don't talk about the children. We don't talk about anything.

Direct message; Zamira @ rebel war

You have children?

ZAMIRA: Yes. I have two. Basinah is thirteen. Issam is five.

KATIE: What if something happens to you? What if you'd been killed tonight?

ZAMIRA: This war wasn't my idea. Things happen to us and we do the best we can.

KATIE: But your husband is fighting. Surely that's enough! Aren't you afraid something will happen to your children?

ZAMIRA: Of course I am. What mother wouldn't be?

KATIE: Then go home! Please! I've no idea what kind of mum I'll turn out to be but I already know I: could never leave her.

ZAMIRA: For years, I thought the same. The most important thing to me was my family. I had to keep them safe no matter what.

KATIE: How come you changed your mind?

ZAMIRA: My husband, Hamza, left for the frontline. He talked about duty and responsibility. A better future for our country. Our children's country.

KATIE: He made you go with him?

ZAMIRA: No. In early spring, a girl was raped and beaten. I kept my head down and did nothing. At home, I couldn't look at my daughter anymore.

KATIE: But it wasn't your fault.

ZAMIRA: I've never felt so ashamed. I couldn't live inside my skin. I couldn't sleep.

KATIE: (Reading) Zamira's blog. Home four months ago. Hamza has been back for seven days. The children hang on to him like he's an exiled king, restored to his throne. He shows me how to use the gun. He makes me go over every action again and again until it is as natural and instinctive as driving a car or making love. I see my gun propped against the chair beside our bed. I can no longer ignore the rising sun. The shadows are changing. I wake Hamza with a kiss pressed onto his lips. It's almost time to leave: to hold our children tightly against us one more time and breathe deeply their skin so we can carry it with us like a precious perfume. I make list after mental list of things I've forgotten to say: remind Granddad Kahil that Issam needs to go to the toilet before bed or he will wet himself; that Basinah gets terrible period pains and needs to take some pills; that there might be times when we can't be in touch but that the three of them should stick together and be brave.

ZAMIRA: Compose new tweet to

katie @ katie D

Are you still awake?

KATIE: Yeah. Are you?

ZAMIRA: Just about. Send me a photo of your baby. Please.

Katie gets off the bed and moves round to take a photo for Zamira. The flash disturbs the baby.

KATIE: (Panics) She's waking up. Zamira! What do I do?

ZAMIRA: It's ok. Just pick her up. She won't break. Children are tougher than they look.

KATIE: The sun's coming up. My Mum will be here soon.

ZAMIRA: Zamira's blog. East of Damascus.

Today: Morning brings with it the business of breakfast, fresh bandages, pills for the pain. The bodies of the dead and dying are brought in and sorted – no Hamza. Maybe he's cheated death again. Maybe soon I will get a tweet or an email from him. Or get to hold my hands against his face. The photo on my phone is blurry: a tiny baby with jet black hair and startled hands. I pull the covers over my head and wait.

KATIE: Retweeted by Katie @ Katie D

Zamira @ rebel war

The baby is silent. A flurry of noise is followed by stillness. Slowly, his mother's broken cries choke the night with grief.

Afterword

Sarah Hehir

The civil uprising in Syria started in the spring of 2011. Initially demanding democratic reforms, the uprising evolved from minor protests to major unrest leading to the emergence of militant opposition movements and massive defections from the Syrian Army. Assad attempted to stop the protests through crackdowns, censorship, concessions and finally troops deployed on the ground. The killing of both protestors and police officers gradually transformed the conflict from a civil uprising to an armed rebellion, and later a full-scale civil war. The rebel Free Syrian Army was created on 29 July 2011, marking the transition into armed insurgency.

While doing research for this play I came across a photo of a female rebel fighter, cleaning her gun with her husband before going to fight in Damascus. This inspired the character of Zamira and the story of a moving connection between two women who seem, at first, to be worlds apart. Twitter has always held a strange magic for me; a few minutes idly flicking through Tweets and Retweets and I can be in a completely unknown world. Telling the whole story through Tweets was a choice of form with obvious limits. I liked the brevity, the pace and the disconnection they gave to the action but found I wanted to relax the structure as the characters opened up to each other. The use of Zamira's blog means that her life and story are more fully explored. With all of the positives and negatives of social media, *Echoes Through the Dust* ultimately celebrates the internet as a medium to connect disparate lives.

Part VI

Be yourself, everyone else is already taken

15 *Coconut Diaries*

Stella Ajayi

Characters

AMBER, *Black-British, female, 21, student. Insecure, but also quirky and willing to learn new things.*
TOBI, *Black-British, male, 22, student. Playful and arrogant.*
LINDA, *Black-British, female, 22, student. Confident and boisterous.*
CHRIS, *White-British, male, 21, student. Comes across as disingenuous, as he often code switches throughout the play. Appears confident but is actually rather insecure.*

Note

(–) at the end of a line indicates being cut off.
(…) indicates where speech trails off.
(Beat) indicates a brief break in the dialogue.

Original production details

Coconut Diaries was commissioned and produced by Little Pieces of Gold at Southwark Playhouse on 10 June 2018.

The cast was as follows:

AMBER	Alisha Artry
TOBI	Deenie Davies
LINDA	Maymuna Abdi
CHRIS	Robert Thorpe-Wood
Director:	Annie Mwampulo
Assistant Directors:	Elizabeth Hollingshead and Michaela Shaw

Scene One

Amber is waiting outside a lecture hall, scrolling through her phone. She has her note book in the other hand, resting underneath her arm, with a back pack on her shoulder. Tobi enters, wearing a long camel coloured jacket, a black turtle neck jumper and a faded high top. He is wearing boat shoes and grey skinny jeans and strolls onstage in a 'cool' suave manner. He looks around briefly before noticing Amber and heads towards her with a cheeky look on his face. He looks her up and down from behind.

TOBI: (Clears throat and in a Nigerian/West African accent) My sister my sister! How are you doin' this fine, fine day?

Amber turns around to acknowledge him briefly, then turns back to her phone.

AMBER: Jesus.

TOBI: Not quite, but close enough.

AMBER: I didn't think my mum would send a Nigerian to spy on me this early into the degree.

TOBI: A-ha … Fellow Naija? Perfect! I need a favour.

AMBER: A favour? Sorry I don't even know your na –

TOBI: Tobi! T-O-B-I. It stands for Taking over big-time init! Anyway, I couldn't help but notice that you look like you have your shit together, and I, apparently do not since I have pretty much missed every lecture so far this year.

AMBER: And you want me to, what, help you?

TOBI: Such a kind offer! I don't even know your na –

AMBER: Amber. It's Amber. But guess what Mr Man, I'm not going to. I already know you've scouted me out as your fellow negro in this town and you therefore think, no, EXPECT me to give up my emotional and intellectual labour to ensure that you pass this degree. If you don't get out of here with your bullshit patriarchy….

TOBI: Wow, okay. Now I am certain you would be the perfect essay writer. How have you already given me a full BBC Bitesize run down of my behaviour? I mean I am not really surprised; black girls are forever giving me attitude.

Tobi checks his watch.

AMBER: Attitude … Attitude?! I'm not like other black girls, Kanye. How'd you think I got myself on this degree in the first place?

TOBI: 'I'm not like other black girls' that's what they all say. And since when did other black girls NOT go uni? (Kisses teeth) You and your respectability politics – (Nigerian accent) Ger out, jor! (Reaches into his jacket and pulls out a business card) Listen, I'm running late, I've got a date with a blondie in Dalston. Was with her a couple weeks ago. When I tell you she gives a whole other meaning to the word head master, my lord … anyway, all my details are on there, if you decide to help a brother out one day then it would be much appreciated.

Amber takes the card from him.

AMBER: You're insane. You're disgusting, yo –
TOBI: -And you're going to Hollywood!

Amber stares at him coldly.

TOBI: American Idol, you're not a fan? Fine, fine.

Tobi takes his sunglasses from his pocket and puts them on, exits leaving Amber in dismay.

Scene Two

A house party – a table full of snacks and drinks. Hip hop music gently plays in the background. Amber and Linda are dressed up, scanning the room.

AMBER: And so it begins, I fucking knew this place would be a 'black only' get together. Fuck my actual life.
LINDA: Just relax I'm sure you're gonna have a good time – have a drink.
AMBER: Have a drink? You already know how low my alcohol tolerance is!
LINDA: Come on, it'll loosen you up.
AMBER: Loosen me up for what?

Beat.

AMBER: Oh my god. You're planning on getting me laid tonight, aren't you? Is that what you meant by loosen up?
LINDA: No you weirdo, just chill out. Everyone can tell you're super nervous.
AMBER: No, everyone can tell that I do not belong here.
LINDA: You're black, Amber. Or did you forget that? You need to drop out of that Michael Jackson school of race you've enrolled yourself in, girl.

Amber notices Chris entering the party, and quickly grabs Linda's arm in excitement.

AMBER: Oh my god, is that....
LINDA: Yup, your 'white boy' crush.
AMBER: He's even more beautiful in real life ... I feel like I've only ever experienced him through my Instagram feed and vibrator.
LINDA: Definitely didn't need to know that, thanks.
AMBER: It's funny that he's at a party like this though. I mean, who would he even know here?
LINDA: Maybe he's on his gap yah and wants to save one of us, and then take us back to Africa in some strange reverse white saviour complex?
AMBER: Not funny!
LINDA: It wasn't a joke, it was an observation. I'm writing a new play ... I call it: 'being white: a concept'. Ooh hello Mr Drake look-a-like, mmm-hmm....

Linda walks away. Chris approaches Amber who is now alone.

CHRIS: Hey, you're on my course, right?
AMBER: (Gulps down drink) Erm, yeah, Chris was it?
CHRIS: Yeah, and you are?
AMBER: Amber.
CHRIS: Amber? Wow that's a pretty white name, isn't it?
AMBER: I mean, it's not quite Gertrude, is it?
CHRIS: Yeah but it's definitely not Shaniqua.
AMBER: Shaniqua! That's a good one. I like that, you're funny. Has anyone ever told you that, like you should totally do stand-up or something.

Chris smiles and looks smug. He runs his hand through his hair. Snoop Dogg's 'Drop it Like it's Hot' starts to play. The volume increases slightly.

CHRIS: Thanks. Oh, man I love this song.
AMBER: What song is it?
CHRIS: You don't know Snoop Dogg?
AMBER: Yeah of course I do, I just don't really listen to him that much, more of a Bob Dylan fan.
CHRIS: Bob Dylan?
AMBER: I mean I know he's old school but I think I'm just an old soul! You're not a fan of his?

Chris' phone rings. He reaches for his pocket and looks at the screen.

CHRIS: Sorry, I gotta take this.

Chris answers his phone.

CHRIS: Yo, yo, yo, what's up Tyrell? Did you get that buff ting's number then? Yo, her booty was next level, I can't believe you're gonna hit that. (places a hand over phone and resumes normal accent to speak to Amber) Ever so sorry for the inconvenience caused, please accept my apologies.
AMBER: (Surprised) No worries.

Chris smiles at her and exits. Linda returns with a bottle of gin in her hand, frustrated.

AMBER: Well, how'd it go with Mr Hotline Bling?
LINDA: He doesn't date black girls.
AMBER: What? How do you know that?
LINDA: Looked me dead in the eye and went 'sorry, I'm not into black girls'. I was like: 'you're not into black girls? Huh, that's interesting. Do you love your mum 'cause I'm pretty sure she was blackety black.' Then he just rolled his eyes and walked away. Unbelievable! He wasn't even that cute to

be honest. I'm sure his head game would have been shit as well, saved my clit a whole load of grief with that one.

Beat.

LINDA: I'm not sure how long I wanna be here to be honest. He's put me right off men!

AMBER: Don't worry, there are plenty of options here, and you're stunning. You'll be fine.

LINDA: Thanks hun. How did it go with Ed Sheeran?

Amber goes over to the drinks/snacks table. She starts picking at crisps but doesn't eat them. Linda follows her.

AMBER: Meh, could've been worse.

LINDA: What do you mean? Jesus what did he say to you?

AMBER: Nothing crazy! I mean, you like Bob Dylan, right?

LINDA: Bob Dylan, which one is that again?

Linda plays air guitar and starts singing intro to 'Living on a Prayer' by Jon Bon Jovi.

AMBER: Nope, that's Bon Jovi. Never mind. Black people aren't monoliths. We're multi layered, aren't we? I can like twerking just as much as I like Bob Dylan. Since when was there a measurement for blackness?

Linda leans into Amber closely.

LINDA: Amber, that was beautiful. Quick question … that weed that was going around earlier, did you have some without me, or?

AMBER: Oh my god, you're not serious. I am going home. I need to study for that essay that's due on Tuesday.

Amber moves away.

LINDA: Amber, wait! You can't have it all for yourself!

Linda runs after her. Chris runs into them before they reach the exit.

CHRIS: Ladies! Leaving already?

Chris reaches into his pocket to show the girls a stash of white powder in a plastic sealant.

CHRIS: Wanna have some fun?

AMBER: Erm … H-have you heard of the lord Jesus Christ?

CHRIS: What, is that a new strain of angel dust or something?

AMBER: No. I mean the man who is here to redeem us of all our sins.

LINDA: (Whispers to Amber) Where are you going with this?

CHRIS: Erm … no, I'm not religious.

AMBER: That's a shame; you should really look upon him some time. He is always here to help people through hard times, especially addiction.

Amber grabs Linda's arm.

AMBER: Excuse us, we just realised how late we are for bible study, have a good one!

CHRIS: Oh, right … see ya.

Linda turns to Chris before following Amber.

LINDA: Please don't tell anyone she just said that.

Linda and Amber exit.

Scene Three

Tobi and Chris each have a bottle of alcohol in one hand. Chris has his elbow on Tobi's shoulder.

CHRIS: And then she went 'Do you listen to Bob Dylan?' That's when I lost it bro. I lost it!

TOBI: She is weird as hell. I mean, I knew a few coconuts from school like her. Always trying to do the most to get some white dick. 'Oh, I love Coldplay. Oh K-pop is everything … black men are all ghetto and can't provide for me!'

CHRIS: She's not wrong though! Black men forever having kids with loads of different women and going on Maury to claim they're not the father. Hilarious.

Chris starts drinking from his bottle. Tobi looks pensive.

TOBI: (Jokingly) Well I like to think I'm the exception to the rule.

CHRIS: You sure you don't have mystery kids running around town?

TOBI: Shut up!

Tobi receives a text. He looks at his phone to see the message. Chris looks over his shoulder.

CHRIS: Oh, hello, who's that from then? Holly? (Reading message) 'So when are you bringing that big black dick over here?'

Tobi removes his phone from Chris' gaze and puts it back into his pocket.

CHRIS: Wow … she wants you like crazy!

TOBI: Maybe. Hey you want another drink?

CHRIS: Nah I'm good, I'm gonna go out for a cigarette though. Catch you in a bit.

Chris exits. Linda enters looking around as if she is trying to find something. She spots Tobi making himself a drink. She turns back around and pretends to look for something. Tobi notices and makes over.

TOBI: Linda … Linda, you alright? You lost something?

LINDA: Sorry, I don't talk to black men who don't want anything to do with black women.

TOBI: Alright, fair enough. Funny though cause your home girl doesn't seem to want to fuck with black men either.

Linda now faces Tobi.

LINDA: Excuse me?

TOBI: You heard me. She's out here pursuing Chris, listening to rock music. Couldn't stop rolling her eyes when she was speaking to me.

LINDA: Funny that. You really don't know anything about her and you're making all these assumptions just because she didn't wanna do your home-work for you?

TOBI: It's more than that. It's like she forgets she's black sometimes.

LINDA: What does that even mean?

TOBI: You know what it means.

LINDA: To be black? What does it mean to be black to you then?

TOBI: Not taking shit from anyone. Not letting European ideas about beauty corrupt your mind.

LINDA: Oh really? Is that why you only date white girls, you've got a corrupted mind?

TOBI: Alright Erykah Badu, your third eye is doing the most right now.

Tobi starts walking away. Linda follows him.

LINDA: Answer me then! Why did you tell me you don't date black girls earlier? You seemed like you had a great answer for me before I told you what's what. I know for a fact I have never heard Amber say that she doesn't date black guys.

TOBI: You're acting like you don't know the answer. But that's fine. All I know is black women are long. White women don't play about. Simple as that. It's always good when they have a body, I won't lie; that's one thing I miss about you lot. But to be honest I date all girls, I can't help that all the white women match with me on Tinder.

LINDA: You can like what you like without shitting on black girls in the process you know!

TOBI: Oh my God, who's shitting on black girls, man?

LINDA: Alright, you know what? I've exhausted myself enough and I haven't even found what I came here for so I'm gonna go. But before I do, I have two words for you – 'sunken place'.

Linda exits. Tobi exits shortly after.

Scene Four

Graduation day. All celebrating and dressed for the occasion – Amber, Linda, Toby and Chris are all stood with a glass of champagne.

AMBER: We did it! We did it! All that studying, sleepless nights, 9 am lectures has finally come to this. What did you get in the end?

TOBI: A First. And a girlfriend.

Tobi takes his phone out and shows Amber her picture.

AMBER: Oh wow, double congrats. Where is she from?

TOBI: Ghana.

AMBER: That's surprising. Aren't you –

TOBI: – 'Into white girls?' What 'cause I dated that one girl earlier in the year? You don't think I went on a spiritual and mental journey of decolonising my mind? I'm over all that now. My girl is waiting for me at home, don't watch that!

AMBER: No, I meant that I'm surprised she's Ghanaian, 'cause you're Nigerian. Isn't the jollof rice issue gonna keep you up at night?

CHRIS: Jollof rice issue! Oh, man, classic!

AMBER: I'm happy for you though, she seems great.

LINDA: (To Amber) What about you, jor! Did you get onto the master's program or not?

TOBI: Master's program? Shit, you don't be wasting no time, do you?

LINDA: (In Nigerian/West African accent) You think she is wasting her time gallivanting with men when she is going to change the world?

AMBER: I got on!

LINDA: Woo-hoo that's my girl!

CHRIS: What's the Master's in?

AMBER: Neuroscience.

TOBI: Neuroscience? Fuck me.

AMBER: I'm good thanks, we all know your track record.

LINDA: She's gonna hunt down white people, take their bodies and plant our brains into them.

CHRIS: W-what, like, 'Get Out'?

AMBER: Yep.

They all laugh.

LINDA: Told you she was gonna change the world!

Ends.

Afterword

Stella Ajayi

Having a degree in psychology has meant that I have always been interested in the complexities of the human condition. As a second-generation Nigerian born and raised in London I'm also aware of the predicaments that can come from being an ethnic minority living in the UK. I therefore wanted *Coconut Diaries* to be a short exploration into these factors through the lens of university students. Specifically, I wanted to show some ways in which black people are affected by, and engage in, internalised racism. Internalised racism can come in many different forms and *Coconut Diaries* explores this – through preferences for dating outside of your race (failing to see the beauty in dating people from your own race) and tendencies towards respectability politics. I wrote *Coconut Diaries* to let the world know that black people are not monoliths; no matter how many stereotypes you see of us, we as individuals will always define our own blackness.

16 *Fox*

Sarah Kosar

Characters

SUSAN, *a confident and relentlessly driven young woman who loves to perform and be watched*
CHARLOTTE, *a shy, supportive and attentive young woman who is easily influenced and is in awe of people with talent*

Notes

(…) indicates where speech trails off.
(/) indicates the point where the immediately following dialogue interrupts.
(Pause) indicates where there is a thought process happening.
Timescale: 1998 to 2006 (8 to 16 years old).
Setting: A small town on the east coast of America between 1998 and 2006. The type of town where everyone knows everyone, and no one ever becomes a somebody. The actors playing the roles can be of any age range.

Original production details

Fox was commissioned and produced by Little Pieces of Gold at Southwark Playhouse on 24 November 2013.

The cast was as follows:

> CHARLOTTE   Alison Campbell
> SUSAN   Meghan Leslie
>
> Director: Anthony Almeida

CHARLOTTE: **1998**. Sometimes you don't know what you want to be when you grow up. But sometimes you have someone that helps you. This is the year I became a fox.
SUSAN: Fox.
CHARLOTTE: Fox.
SUSAN: Fox.

BOTH: Fox.

CHARLOTTE: "Susan and The Fox." That's a really, really good name. How'd you come up with it?

SUSAN: It just came to me.

CHARLOTTE: Where from?

SUSAN: A place called inspiration.

CHARLOTTE: Can I visit someday?

SUSAN: Maybe.

CHARLOTTE: You're the smartest best friend.

SUSAN: And you're the nicest best friend.

Susan and Charlotte high five and do their secret handshake.

CHARLOTTE: So "Susan and The Fox." That's our name?

SUSAN: And we're sticking to it.

CHARLOTTE: Oh my god. I have an idea.

SUSAN: Tell me.

CHARLOTTE: What about … "Susan AND Charlotte"?

SUSAN: We need to be famous. No. We will be famous. "Susan and The Fox" is the name of famous people. Soo….

CHARLOTTE: Awesome! Am I the fox?

SUSAN: Yeah, I'm gonna get you a mop for a tail and a headband with ears.

Susan hands Charlotte a tail and a headband with ears. Charlotte prepares herself to be crowned the fox. Susan puts them on her.
    Charlotte makes fox noises.

CHARLOTTE: You have the coolest ideas. And what do I do?

SUSAN: This.

Susan teaches a "fox" dance to Charlotte to do behind her. Susan stands in front of Charlotte.

SUSAN: And I'll sing in front of you. And I'm going to write a song to the theme of "My Heart Will Go On" and we will be the next Celine Dion. Ready?

CHARLOTTE: You think? We will?

SUSAN: Totally. And that will give us eight years until we are 16 and famous like Britney Spears. I've worked out the math. People become famous at 16. Brains!

CHARLOTTE: But Britney Spears doesn't have a fox?

SUSAN: We're like Josie and the Pussycats. You're the pussycat, but a fox. C'mon shake your tail. Shake it.

Charlotte shakes her fox tail. She waits for Susan's response. Susan cheers.

SUSAN: You're really talented. And blonde. That helps. A lot.

CHARLOTTE: Baby Spice and Britney Spears are blonde. And Pamela Anderson.

SUSAN: Exactly. You've got the hang of this!

CHARLOTTE: Will we have to leave home?

SUSAN: At 16 to perform for millions of people. Yeah.

CHARLOTTE: But I've only ever spent the night at your house.

SUSAN: It'll be just like that but on a moving bus.

CHARLOTTE: Okay, could we pack your spice girls' night light?

SUSAN: Totally! But first we need to make a lifetime promise.

CHARLOTTE: Lifetime! That's a long time.

SUSAN: Like forever. Do you want to be famous? Look at me. Put your arm here, and your eyes looking right into my eyes.

Charlotte and Susan stare at each other.

CHARLOTTE: Do you?

SUSAN: Yes, and you want to be famous too.

CHARLOTTE: Yes, I want to be famous too.

SUSAN: Louder.

CHARLOTTE: I WANT TO BE FAMOUS TOO.

SUSAN: Fantastic. Tremendous. Sign here. It says that you will always be my backup fox dancer and that you won't get your ears pierced until we are 13 years old and can do it together at Claire's at the Clearview Mall.

Susan hands Charlotte a pen and paper.

CHARLOTTE: Not until 13? I wanted to get them/at 10.

SUSAN: Yeah, it will be on MTV then. If you want/to be on MTV.

CHARLOTTE: Hmmm….

SUSAN: Plus foxes look prettier with pierced ears when they're older. Don't you want to be pretty. And famous. And foxtastic?

CHARLOTTE: Okay, cool.

Charlotte signs the paper. She hands the paper back to Susan.

1999. Our first big gig. You don't know the meaning of money until someone shows you.

SUSAN: Just go around and ask everyone here for five dollars.

CHARLOTTE: Why?

SUSAN: Because that's what we charge.

CHARLOTTE: They all look really busy/

SUSAN: They have money in their pockets. Go ask. This is the music business.

CHARLOTTE: I'm scared.

SUSAN: We can do a practice round.

CHARLOTTE: Okay.

Susan waits for Charlotte.

SUSAN: Ask me. Pretend I'm that lady in the dress with the little teapots all over it.

Charlotte looks at the woman with the dress and then back to Susan.

CHARLOTTE: (Whispering) Hi, um, Hi. Can I – I have five – Can I have five dollars?
SUSAN: No!
CHARLOTTE: Okay.

Charlotte walks away.

SUSAN: That's not okay. Tell them who you are and what we're doing. C'mon!
CHARLOTTE: We are "Susan and The Fox" and I'm the fox. We are going to perform for you. It's five dollars. Can I have five dollars?

Susan just looks at Charlotte.

CHARLOTTE: We are "Susan and The Fox" and I'm the fox. We are going to perform for you.
It's five dollars. Can I have five dollars?

Susan doesn't do anything.

Please?

Susan shakes Charlotte's head.

SUSAN: Foxes are more stern. You have to be stern. Make a fist when you ask.

Susan looks at Charlotte and raises a stern fist.

SUSAN: Five dollars please! "Susan and The Fox" will be performing soon. This is mandatory.

Susan raises her fist. Charlotte digs into her pockets and finds a fiver, she hands it to Susan.

SUSAN: See! That's how it's done.

Susan puts the five dollars in her pocket. Charlotte watches it go into Susan's pocket, and knows it will never return to her.

CHARLOTTE: Okay.

SUSAN: I'm the bank for "Susan and The Fox". That's all. Have you been practicing your tail move when I sing the bridge?

Charlotte spins in a circle so her tail goes out.

SUSAN: Better. And again.

Charlotte spins again.

CHARLOTTE: There are some girls at my school that are starting a band too!
SUSAN: They aren't any good.
CHARLOTTE: How do you know?
SUSAN: Nobody could be better than us!
CHARLOTTE: Can't everyone be famous?
SUSAN: No! It's like heaven, and there is only room for the best.
CHARLOTTE: Oh. They asked me to be one of the singers. They're called Destiny's Grandchildren.

Susan pulls on Charlotte's ear headband.

SUSAN: What did you say to them?
CHARLOTTE: I said no. That I couldn't because I'm a fox.

Susan lets go of Charlotte's ear.

SUSAN: Good. That's our competition. You can't hang around with the competition.
CHARLOTTE: I wish you went to my school.
SUSAN: I wish you were Catholic and could come to mine.
CHARLOTTE: Are all Catholics as talented as you?
SUSAN: No. Now when they bring the cake out, help my grandma with her hearing aid so she can hear us real loud and then let's sing Wannabe.
CHARLOTTE: Okay.

Charlotte looks at Susan and she starts practicing the routine. It does not look good. Susan pulls Charlotte to the side.

SUSAN: Let's start again! Ah five, six, a five six seven eight....
CHARLOTTE: **2000**. Selling Girl Scout Cookies.
SUSAN: If we get everyone on this road to buy a box and then the road down there, and the one further down there, then we will win. Totally win!
CHARLOTTE: Awesome!
SUSAN: Do you like winning?
CHARLOTTE: I guess/I do.
SUSAN: We love winning!

Susan and Charlotte high five and do their secret handshake.

SUSAN: I mean I'll win, but I'll totally let you use the telescope.
CHARLOTTE: It's a telescope?
SUSAN: Yep. Whoever in my troupe sells the most cookies gets a telescope.
CHARLOTTE: But wait, what do I get?
SUSAN: To use the telescope.
CHARLOTTE: It's really dark now.
SUSAN: Which is why we need the telescope.
CHARLOTTE: We should go home.
SUSAN: No.
CHARLOTTE: We told your Mom we would be home at sunset.
SUSAN: My Mom wants us to win, she'll understand.
CHARLOTTE: Do you have a flashlight?
SUSAN: No, let's keep knocking on doors.
CHARLOTTE: What if we get kidnapped? That's what happens when it's dark.
SUSAN: The real question is, what if we don't get that telescope?
CHARLOTTE: **2001**. Sometimes you need to watch the best to learn from them.
SUSAN: Just watch me.

Susan does a dance for Charlotte. Susan gets on the ground. She kicks her legs up. She watches Charlotte watching her.

SUSAN: If you've been watching the music videos like I've asked you, it's really
    in to get on the ground and dance. Like in Oops I Did It Again. Did
    you see?
CHARLOTTE: Yeah. I don't have to wear that red catsuit, do I?
SUSAN: No, no of course not. I will. Here get on the floor and try.

Charlotte hesitantly gets on the floor and tries to perform some lay down dancing.

SUSAN: And this one is really good.

Susan gets up and turns around and wraps her arms around her and moves them around (so it looks like she is kissing someone). Charlotte starts to do it but then stops.

SUSAN: (She whispers) It's sexual.
CHARLOTTE: Do foxes have to be sexual?
SUSAN: Not if you're not ready.
CHARLOTTE: I'm just going to wag my tail.

Charlotte wags her tail.

CHARLOTTE: **2002.** Mother's Day.

SUSAN: People like famous people that love their families. If we make this the best Mother's Day, then our Moms will say nice things when they're interviewed on TV about us. Good publicity.

CHARLOTTE: I do love my family. They are really/nice.

SUSAN: See you already know how to answer interview questions.

CHARLOTTE: I do?

SUSAN: Did you get some money?

CHARLOTTE: I thought we were going to use the money we got from your Aunt's nursing home?

SUSAN: That's all gone.

CHARLOTTE: How? Where did it go?

SUSAN: I bought some new CDs.

CHARLOTTE: What about my half? I have half.

SUSAN: You get to listen to them with me.

CHARLOTTE: But they aren't mine.

SUSAN: I'm sorry. Did your Dad get the cake stuff?

CHARLOTTE: Yep.

SUSAN: Moms love cake.

CHARLOTTE: I love cake.

Susan and Charlotte read the cake instructions.

SUSAN: Two egg whites.

CHARLOTTE: What are egg whites?

SUSAN: The white part, right?

CHARLOTTE: It's white. So yeah.

SUSAN: Dump out the stuff inside and put the white part in the bowl.

CHARLOTTE: Okay. Will you give me my half of the money?

Susan just looks at Charlotte.

CHARLOTTE: It's not fair.

2003. The Chicken Pox.

SUSAN: Dear Fox, I've got the Chicken Pox. My Mom said we can't play because I've got to stay in my oatmeal bath until it stops. I wanted to give you the CDs to listen to so they are inside this package. I've put them in your mailbox so you don't have to see me all spotty. I'm very spotty. I miss you and your bushy tail and loads of talent. Listen to Genie in the Bottle because I think we can learn a lot from it. You're blonde, so you can really relate to Christina. I'm working on a routine to it when I'm not scratching. I'll teach it to you when I'm better. The CDs are half yours. Sorry. Love your best friend, Susan (from "Susan and The Fox)'

CHARLOTTE: I opened the package. I listened to Genie in the Bottle. I started to scratch. I've got the Chicken Pox now too.

SUSAN: Dear Fox, don't scratch too much, they cause marks. Well at least we aren't alone.

CHARLOTTE: Sometimes you realize your best friend sent you a disease through the mail. She poured her pox in a bottle and it came out like a genie. She was very smart.

SUSAN: No. No./No!

CHARLOTTE: Jennifer's nice.

SUSAN: We need to practice.

CHARLOTTE: Not every single day.

SUSAN: Do you want to be famous?

CHARLOTTE: She just wanted to come over to swim.

SUSAN: You signed a lifetime agreement.

CHARLOTTE: You gave me the Chicken Pox.

SUSAN: I didn't.

CHARLOTTE: You definitely did.

SUSAN: It was probably someone from Destiny's Grandchildren!

CHARLOTTE: You're my best friend and you made me sick.

SUSAN: Why do we need anyone else?

CHARLOTTE: Even famous people have other friends.

SUSAN: Not when they're trying to be famous.

CHARLOTTE: Yeah huh! They interviewed Britney Spears' friends from high school. Two different ones. Two!

SUSAN: But we're "Susan and The Fox."

CHARLOTTE: I'm sorry you don't like any of the Catholics.

SUSAN: They can't see talent because they pray too much.

CHARLOTTE: They shouldn't be mean to you.

SUSAN: Then you shouldn't be mean to me. Don't be their friend....

Susan starts to sing "Say You'll Be There" by The Spice Girls to Charlotte.

SUSAN: (Sings) I'm giving you everything. All that joy can bring, this I swear, and all that I want from you....

Susan pauses.

CHARLOTTE: (Sings) Is a promise you will be there.

Susan walks away from Charlotte.

I'm waiting for Susan to start talking to me again. I've been waiting since last Tuesday, and today is Monday. I put notes in her mailbox. Not even with diseases on them. I go to Jennifer's birthday party. I don't tell Susan. But I take my tail off. I don't stand behind anyone when the music starts playing. Everyone is in the same line. Everyone does the same motion. I'm not behind anyone. And I'm first in line for pin the tail on the donkey. I asked the girls there if they were in bands like Danielle and the Donkey, Tammy and the Turtle, and Wilma and the Walrus. No one was a donkey, turtle, walrus or even a fox. Just me.

Charlotte puts on earrings.
Susan circles around Charlotte, staring her up and down. Susan gets out their lifetime agreement and crinkles it up and throws it in Charlotte's face.

SUSAN: You signed a lifetime agreement!
CHARLOTTE: I'm sorry.
SUSAN: You promised.
CHARLOTTE: I'm sorry.
SUSAN: We'll never be famous now!
CHARLOTTE: I'm sorry. It was my birthday present.
SUSAN: We were supposed to pierce our ears together. And do an MTV interview. 'Breaking News'.

CHARLOTTE: I'll still go with you.
SUSAN: I don't want to now.
CHARLOTTE: Yes, you do.
SUSAN: I mean maybe this is a traumatic time I can write a song about, but that is the only good thing about this. This is very very sad.
CHARLOTTE: I don't know what to say.
SUSAN: Do you have a new friend? Jennifer?
CHARLOTTE: No.
SUSAN: Do you?
CHARLOTTE: No.
SUSAN: You're not acting like my fox.
CHARLOTTE: Maybe I'm Charlotte.
SUSAN: You know what I mean.
CHARLOTTE: Can I sing a verse?
SUSAN: You've pierced your ears and now you want a verse?
CHARLOTTE: I've never had a verse so....
SUSAN: You like my voice.
CHARLOTTE: I like your voice but do you like mine?
SUSAN: Kind of.
CHARLOTTE: Do you like my voice?
SUSAN: You're the fox.
CHARLOTTE: Do you like my dancing?
SUSAN: You shake your tail well.
CHARLOTTE: Do you think I'm talented?

Pause.

SUSAN: You're half of "Susan and The Fox."

Pause.

CHARLOTTE: But there's no Charlotte in there?

Pause.

2006. I'm sorry. That like totally sucks.
SUSAN: They said I wasn't "strong enough."
CHARLOTTE: You're too good for them.
SUSAN: I didn't make high school chorus. That means I'm bad. Football players
    with crackly voices even make high school chorus.
CHARLOTTE: You're really good.
SUSAN: You don't have to say that/
CHARLOTTE: You are.
SUSAN: They don't think I am.
CHARLOTTE: But I do.
SUSAN: Charlotte, maybe I'm not that good. Maybe I've just been delusional/
CHARLOTTE: You are/good.
SUSAN: Why didn't you tell me I'm not good?
CHARLOTTE: Because I think you are.
SUSAN: No.
CHARLOTTE: Yes.
SUSAN: Are you the only one?
CHARLOTTE: Sing for me.
SUSAN: You don't have to say that.
CHARLOTTE: I want to watch you.

Susan starts to sing "My Heart Will Go On," but stops after a line.

SUSAN: Sometimes you realize you're 16 and you aren't famous and you haven't
    been a super good or nice person. That you aren't Celine Dion but a bit
    more like a sinking ship.
CHARLOTTE: We're Britney's age at the release of "Baby One More Time."
SUSAN: We're 16. We aren't famous. We aren't Susan and –
CHARLOTTE: – The Fox.
SUSAN: The Fox is what they call Charlotte's friend Jennifer now because she is
    really hot.
CHARLOTTE: We still live next to each other, and now we go to the same high
    school.
SUSAN: And we still learn all the new routines.
CHARLOTTE: And I still stand behind her.
SUSAN: And sometimes we'll stand in the same line. With a bunch of other
    people too.
CHARLOTTE: And –
SUSAN: We stopped performing.

CHARLOTTE:　But I'll never stop believing in Susan.

SUSAN:　I'm not famous, but one person thinks I should be.

CHARLOTTE:　And I don't think I'll ever stop thinking that. And maybe one day she will be.

SUSAN:　But maybe one day I'll move somewhere new, and find another fox and that fox will tell another and another and they'll all sit in a theatre and watch me and they'll think, that is someone famous.

Pause.

And that was "Susan and The Fox" performing. That will be five dollars.

Susan puts her hand out.

Afterword

Sarah Kosar

Fox is one of the most personal plays I've ever written. I was inspired to write it based upon my experiences of bullying and my own relationship with my best friend growing up. *Fox* is set very much in nondescript small-town America, the type of place where there isn't loads to do or mountains of entertainment, so the power of imagination, storytelling and even delusion is vital to be able to get you through day-to-day life, especially if you don't have a lot of friends. It's a place where everyone knows each other, and will continue to for the whole of their lives. When one is bullied as a child in this type of environment, a sense of overblown ego or confidence can grow quite rapidly. This is often because one must find a way to invent a world that is so far from the one they are living in day to day in order to find, develop, and keep a positive sense of self. A place where they exist without the definitions others have created for them. The play examines the relationship between reality and fantasy, and what happens when you veer too far on one side. You may risk becoming the bully instead of the bullied and even lose the one person who sees you fully in reality and not the fantasy you create. Set between 1998 and 2006, the play also plays with the act of performance, both to oneself, others and to the future you hope to reach.

17 *Soon in the 4ciable Future*

Elizabeth Kwenortey

Characters

PATRICIA, *early twenties, Black-British.*
TIANA, *early twenties, British-Jamaican.*
HOLLY, *early twenties, Mixed British-Jamaican.*
LAURYN, *early twenties, British-Nigerian.*

Notes

(–) at the end of a line indicates being cut off.
(…) indicates where speech trails off.
(/) indicates the point where the immediately following dialogue interrupts.

Original production details

Soon in the 4ciable Future was commissioned and produced by Little Pieces of Gold at Canal Café Theatre from the 12 to 14 March 2018.

The cast was as follows:

LAURYN	Afua Ansah
TIANA	Ishara Bilson-Graham
HOLLY	Lou Mussington
PATRICIA	Rachel Shobande
Director:	Monique Touko

Patricia's bedroom. Patricia sits in front of her bedroom vanity. Tiana is on a chair. Holly sits on the bed next to Lauryn.

PATRICIA: LADIES! Look, I'm tryna find me a man. Yeah, I've been patient you know? Being a Christian and all of that, but come on, I want to get married and have a nice guy explore my guts!

TIANA: WOAH okay, I see the sexual frustration has reached a new high.

PATRICIA: I have waited and prayed, got a degree, got a job, ignored the many micro-aggressions thrown my way and not retaliated with murder.

HOLLY: Same, I'm in need of a good man too.

LAURYN: I swear you had a good man but he walked in on you cheating with his flatmate.

Lauryn takes a sip of her drink.

PATRICIA: It's hard out here for a pimp. But good news ladies – as you can see by me getting ready, I'm going somewhere special tonight. I've got a date!

TIANA: Oh girl have fun and remember health class in year nine – make sure it's wrapped up before h –

PATRICIA: Excuse you I'm still waiting till marriage for that. I'm excited and nervous, I don't even know where to begin.

HOLLY: Oh, maybe start with your appearance?

LAURYN: You're telling your friend that the first thing she should work on is her appearance? Great friendship, very supportive.

HOLLY: You can borrow my Zara jacket, it would suit you. Plus I've worn it out anyway.

LAURYN: Aww … her worn out second hand clothing! Always the philanthropist.

TIANA: Mother Teresa eat your heart out.

HOLLY: What are you gonna do with your hair?

Tiana, Patricia and Lauryn all look at each other in silence.

LAURYN: You're like everyone I hated at Edinburgh rolled into one. I know you can't help it but just be happy that it was Pat who met you first and was willing to look past alladat 'cause I would've had none. Of. It.

PATRICIA Wait hold on … what's wrong with how my hair is now?

HOLLY: Isn't that a bit full on for a first date – why not just straighten it? You have to try a little before you show your true self, and then just when he gets comfortable, that's when you TRAP HIM!

Holly laughs by herself. She tries to get a high-five from Tiana but she doesn't react.

TIANA: More than a minute with none of your rich white friends round here and you forget where you are?

HOLLY: Well I just mean that –

PATRICIA: Pretty, but by European standards. I want someone who doesn't care if my hair is a "mess" because he wants to mess it up some more … if you know what I am saying … (speaking quickly and getting quieter) 'cause we will be wearing helmets whilst we ride our bikes down the road.

TIANA: BIKES? I thought you were tryna ride something else. Plus, if he's got a problem with your hair he should take it up with his mother, father, grand-parents and keep going till he reaches God.

Lauryn impersonating African American preachers.

LAURYN: Will a man argue with God?

TIANA: No suh'!

ALL laughing.

PATRICIA: He's black anyway – black black – so I can only hope it won't be an issue.

TIANA: Hope and pray, especially remembering the "black" folk you guys met at uni.

LAURYN: Rich black people are a problem of their own.

HOLLY: What's wrong with the black boys at uni? They all seemed lovely.

LAURYN: Don't get me wrong, the self-hatred amongst the rich black girls was hella evident, going the extra way not to be the angry black girl.

TIANA: Which you are doing a great job disproving by the way.

HOLLY: I wouldn't be surprised if you told me that she came out of the womb angry.

LAURYN: As I was saying. The black boys were of a … different breed. Do you remember Olafemi?

PATRICIA/

LAURYN: Or Francis for short!

LAURYN: That boy's name was Olafemi Onayawhipo Awonswumi. He came over when he was thirteen, so still had his Nigerian accent.

PATRICIA: However –

LAURYN: When Mr Man found his way into one of the bougiest Russell group unis in the UK, where the smell of money –

PATRICIA: And other things –

LAURYN: – radiates down accommodation hallways, Francis, changed it up. (Nigerian accent) "Good afternoon", turned into (fancy English voice) "so lads where we going tonight" I remember when he got angry at a waiter who made us wait longer than others to be seated you could fully hear the accent.

HOLLY: But that happens to loads of people, in different situations, their native accent comes out.

PATRICIA: Yeah, but this was different. I mean we all have a phone voice but I have never seen such an active effort to increase employability.

LAURYN: This Dr Jekyll, Mr Hyde type thing. Plus he was a bit of a hoe and his political views made me itch. ANYWAYS, he told me about his aim of exploring the "native cuisine" – a.k.a. white women before settling with an "African queen".

TIANA: WOW, I mean, if it were the other way round and a white man went around to other countries with such a poor attitude to local women.

ALL stop whatever they are doing and slowly turn their heads to face the audience as if to say "Mhm".

LAURYN: He tried to switch on me. He was like (Nigerian accent) "you black women hate white women anyway … why do you care … you guys are just jealous ... look at your hair for example ... trying to straighten it to match their style".

TIANA: Rah, is this what Russell groups have done to black people? Have them believing that they have transcended race yeah? Well obvs, except you lot. Besides who wants a pussy scared of a little hair anyway?

ALL burst out in laughter.

PATRICIA: Look here, I don't know what is wanted from me. I'm educated at a great institution, have expanded and challenged my mind and I'm in touch with my womanly instincts deep down within my soul.

TIANA: A'ight Erykah Badu. Plus remember we didn't all go to a Russell group uni.

PATRICIA: That was your choice – did you or did you not have the grades? Talkin bout you tryna find Kofis and Jeromes, not James' and Harrys.

LAURYN: But there are some guys who appreciate our hair.

PATRICIA: Where?

Prolonged silence.

PATRICIA: Look at that hesitation. Whenever you lot argue with guys or they 'banter' your looks, what do they go for first?

TIANA: Yeah, but all you have to do is remind them of how their football career never really took off.

HOLLY: My webbed toes –

PATRICIA: PLUS, what about (whispering) white boys.

TIANA: What about them? I know a few white boys that dig an afro. And personally I think that those twenty-year-old white boys who don't dig it should keep their opinions to themselves. They've got about fifteen good years till their cuteness runs out so they should focus on making the most of it rather than voicing their dislike of someone else's natural form.

PATRICIA: I mean how will they react to (gestures to herself) all of this?

HOLLY: Why were you whispering when you said white boys? LOL we know that's what you like. Do you think we are blind?

LAURYN: Whilst me and Tiana were all melting over JLS in secondary school, Pat was tearing up at The Wanted (singing) *"You don't know you're beautiful"*.

PATRICIA: Actually, One Direction.

ALL (EXCEPT PATRICIA): Ahhh.

PATRICIA: I just want a posh rich white boy tryna shake the table like Prince Harry.

TIANA: It's alright if you dig a lil' vanilla. But like I said, fifteen good years then ... meh.

Holly stands up, hesitates to speak.

HOLLY: I didn't mean to knock your confidence Pat, you know I love you. Without you I wouldn't have had anyone when Edinburgh got tough.

LAURYN: I'm not saying I can't see why.

Lauryn sips her drink.

HOLLY: Sometimes I wonder why I hang out with you guys, but believe it or not, you make my day. And by the way, just because there is money doesn't mean there is love. The best things in life are free.

LAURYN: Can someone tell that to Nandos. Last time I went there and tried to get my meal for free I ended up in handcuffs. Plus that's rich coming from a girl born into money.

TIANA: Reminds me of a song, a great song. *"The best things in life are free, but you can give that to the birds and bees I need money!"* (ref: "Money That's What I Want" by Barrett Strong).

LAURYN/

PATRICIA: That's what I want! (beat) I don't know why it took Holly talking about my hair to rattle us so much. Didn't our mothers tell us the same? Straighten your hair, look nice to find a husband?

ALL the girls contemplate for a minute.

HOLLY: I never really heard that, growing up. Well I guess my Dad is a man so it's diff –

TIANA: Oh, your father is black? Is he a Tiger Woods type?

HOLLY: We never spoke to his side. Plus I either had my hair the way it is now or straightened. Was never really an issue. The boys that I dated liked it, said it was exotic.

Lauryn and Tiana groan.

PATRICIA: Okay don't get me wrong guys – this has been a great, great chat … love it, hm yeah do a TED talk! But thanks to Holly – don't worry I still love you girl – I am still unsure about my hair.

HOLLY: Your natural hair is ni –

PATRICIA: Too late for that! Ladies. Ideas, gimme something different.

TIANA: MEN! You realise if you had a girlfriend none of this would be happening.

PATRICIA: You'd still wanna look nice for bae.

LAURYN: Just 'cause you swing that way isn't gonna ensure that a life partner won't tease her about an insecurity.

TIANA: Shouldn't even be an insecurity. It's a part of us. Our natural hair is who we are.

HOLLY: Right on!

Tiana, Lauryn and Patricia all turn to look at Holly.

HOLLY: Have you guys … ever … maybe possibly thought –

PATRICIA: It shouldn't come from you. Have you guys ever thought that maybe we are all overthinking this? Tryna predict his attitude before I have even met the guy?

LAURYN: Ah no, do you need a case study? Have you seen the news? Are you guys that unaware? Want a ticket to Awaresville?

TIANA: Are you gonna talk or keep doing this?

LAURYN: Look at the way the media treated Michelle Obama, and she kept it professional. Didn't see her natural hair in its natural state until they came out of office! Now Melanie, melanin, Melania, lasagne, whatever the new one's name is, she can roll outta bed and they'll call her "sexy" and "bed head".

PATRICIA: I do think there are two sides to it. We have a reason to think the way we do but at the same time, I am so self-conscious.

LAURYN: (Singing) *"I'm telling you oh, that it all falls down."* ("All Falls Down" by Kanye West).

ALL burst out in laughter. Lauryn and Holly stand up to dance.

TIANA: Man I promise, she's so self-conscious. (Under her breath) She's so precious with the peer pressure (to Patricia) she had hair so long that it look like weave, then she cut it all off now she look like Eve –

PATRICIA: HELLO. My hair?

TIANA: Well relax it.

PATRICIA/

LAURYN: Chemical burn.

LAURYN: And time.

HOLLY: Afro?

PATRICIA: If the humidity gets to me it's all over. I'll roll through looking like Sideshow Bob!

TIANA: Use a straightener.

PATRICIA: Heat damage.

TIANA: What about your sister's wig? It's here all ready and prepped.

PATRICIA: I feel like I'm lying; it's not my hair but I am trying to give off the impression that it is. Plus what if we get in a fight and he whips it off?

HOLLY: You're going in circles.

PATRICIA: What?

TIANA: She's right. We've sat here whining, actually whining about how sad it is for us but if you are going to go through all this every time you go on a date you need to ask yourself: is it worth it?

LAURYN: I understand you wanna get hitched all traditional but you need to understand that the simplest way to go through all of this, is by being yourself. Of course you need to care about the physical, but don't over-do it or pretend to be something you're not.

TIANA: Plus, you do know there isn't really that much wrong with wearing wigs, weaves etcetera. It's not only black women that do that. I mean Dolly Parton?

PATRICIA: You guys are right, thanks. I should finish getting ready.

HOLLY: Tell us how it goes.

PATRICIA: I will!

TIANA: Girl you better hurry up. If you were worried about presenting yourself as stereotypically black, you sure have with your lateness!

PATRICIA: Well he's probably late too.

Patricia is left standing alone in the room. She looks at her wig, turns around, hesitates and puts on her wig cap. She then adjusts the wig on her head, puts on her jacket and collects her bag. She looks at herself in the mirror and takes a deep breath. She walks offstage.

PATRICIA: Fuck that!

Patricia throws the wig back onstage.

Ends.

Afterword

Elizabeth Kwenortey

Hair has always been a central symbol within various Black communities. Historically, afro hair and styling has been the target of unfair and prejudice laws seeking to restrict and limit its exposure to the public eye. For example, in the 1700s, the Tigon Laws saw African American women forced to wrap up their hair, and only in 2017 did the American military lifted a hair ban on dreadlocks.

The natural hair movement, encouraging women to keep and maintain the natural kinky and curled hair textures they were born with, has gained ground since the beginning of the twenty-first century but many still find themselves debating whether to wear their hair naturally or to change their hair to conform to a certain standard. This play explores the conflict around maintaining one's natural hair, how it not only affects people on a professional level but also within their personal lives. So whilst the four girls in this play have been successful in their education they feel that their physical appearance may limit their success in relationships.

18   *A Better Pronoun*

Lydia Parker

Characters

JEN, *forties, British.*
TILLY, *15, British.*

Notes

(/) marks the point where the immediately following dialogue interrupts.
(–) at the end of a line indicates being cut off.
(…) at the end of a speech means it trails off. On its own it indicates a pressure or expectation to speak.

Production details

A Better Pronoun was commissioned and produced by Little Pieces of Gold at the Old Red Lion on 18 January 2016.

The cast was as follows:

JEN	Abigail Burdess
TILLY	Rebecca Boey
Director:	Lydia Parker

Jen and Tilly sit at the kitchen table. Jen has a laptop in front of her, in the middle of reading Tilly's homework assignment. Tilly has papers and books spread in front of her but also checks her phone occasionally.

JEN: Pregnant?
TILLY: Yeah.
JEN: How far?
TILLY: Four months. I think.
JEN: Jesus.
TILLY: Yeah.
JEN: Who's the father?

TILLY: Danny. From number 17.

JEN: Danny Wethersfield? But he's tiny; he looks like he's ten years old....

TILLY: He went through a growth spurt. Anyway, they broke up already but she wants to keep the baby.

JEN: Nicola was such a sweet girl.

TILLY: You mean she's not anymore since she's a pregnant teenager?

JEN: Her mother can't be more than thirty.

TILLY: Thirty two. She had Nic at seventeen.

JEN: She probably encouraged her to get pregnant.

TILLY: Mum!

JEN: What? I just don't understand it. What do they teach you in school anyway?

TILLY: You mean in sex ed? I don't know, the usual … how to not get pregnant.

JEN: Well I guess Nicola missed that lesson.

TILLY: To be honest, I missed it. I had piano.

JEN: Oh brilliant. So do I need to worry about you getting pregnant too?

TILLY: Well, Danny Wethersfield is single now. Look, can you please just finish proof-reading my history essay?

JEN: In a minute, this is important. I ought to complain to the school. Fifteen year old girls getting pregnant right under their nose.

TILLY: Whose nose?

JEN: The school's nose.

TILLY: The school's nose? Are you sure you should be correcting my grammar?

JEN: Don't be cheeky.

TILLY: Nic loves babies! It's her choice and she's happy. I think.

JEN: I'll write the school an email.

Jen starts typing.

TILLY: Leave it, please Mum!

JEN: Britain has the highest rate of teenage pregnancy in Europe. Someone has to take responsibility. What exactly do they teach you? In sex education?

TILLY: I don't know. Stuff about condoms.

JEN: Just birth control?

TILLY: And scary STDs. Oh, we saw a film about consent. And an episode of *Skins*.

JEN: So no one actually talks to you? Who teaches it?

TILLY: Mr Evans.

JEN: He's a geography teacher!

TILLY: He seemed really embarrassed showing a room full of girls how to put a condom on a banana. I felt sorry for him. Everyone was giggling.

JEN: They're still doing the condom on a banana?

TILLY: It's put me off bananas for life.

JEN: These girls need a woman teaching them. Sex is about more than not getting pregnant.

TILLY: I had nightmares for weeks about giving birth to little banana shaped babies. And then eating them.

JEN: Can you please take this seriously?

TILLY: Can you please get back to my history essay?

JEN: Which is all about suffragettes! What do you think these women were fighting for?

TILLY: The vote?

JEN: That and their right to an orgasm.

TILLY: Oh okay, let me just rewrite my essay.

JEN: Women in Victorian times were told to lie back and think of England. That pleasure was for men and prostitutes. Things have hardly progressed!

TILLY: Uh…

JEN: No, really, boys learn about sex from porn videos, I read about this in the Guardian. They think women are just there to, you know, give them … gratification. It's disgusting.

TILLY: Yes, so can we not talk about it?

JEN: I mean these boys don't just expect blow jobs, no, they now insist on anal sex! Anal sex! Can you believe thirteen year old boys demanding that their thirteen year old girlfriends have anal sex?

TILLY: Can you please stop saying anal sex?

JEN: They need to be teaching you about what you should expect from a loving relationship. Your father and I –

TILLY: Don't –

JEN: Have always been considerate and caring for each other's needs and –

TILLY: Stop!

JEN: Okay, but please tell me you know that a woman should … sex is a wonderful, amazing experience under the right circumstances, but a lot of women never experience –

TILLY: Orgasms. I know. Mum, I don't want to talk about this with you. I am dying inside right now.

JEN: Okay, so you are aware –

TILLY: Yes, I'm aware.

JEN: But have you –

TILLY: Mum, not appropriate.

JEN: But I want total honesty between us. My mum never told me anything. I learned about periods from some Judy Blume book. I didn't even know how men and women had … intercourse until I was twelve. Go on, laugh.

TILLY: I'm not. (Beat) So how did you think it happened?

JEN: I … I thought they slept together and the sperm somehow wafted to the woman.

TILLY: Wafted?

JEN: Flowed. I don't know. No one ever told me about … penetration and ejaculation!

TILLY: More words I didn't expect to hear from you. Keep 'em coming, Mum.

JEN: I just want to be sure that you don't have screwed up sexual experiences. Like most people in the world.

TILLY: Well, now that I've heard my mum shout anal sex and ejaculation all in one conversation, I think I'm set for life. Look, Mum … my mates and I talk about stuff. Okay? Happy?

JEN: Okay. (Beat) But I still think I should write a letter about sex education –

TILLY: We already did.

JEN: We who?

TILLY: We who? My friends and I. We did it for all the kids younger than us who … who might be really confused and maybe a little scared. The national curriculum has got to change.

JEN: Absolutely! No more bananas, just honest, straight talk about what a woman should expect from a man, and not just orgasms but –

TILLY: Kids need to be educated about gender identity.

JEN: What?

TILLY: I mean, what if a girl is attracted to other girls?

JEN: Oh. (Pause) Well, that's fine, of course, but –

TILLY: Do you remember Alexa Lucas?

JEN: Oh yes, very quirky parents, I always thought her dad was gay, he wore a lot of bracelets and eyeliner –

TILLY: Alexa's going out with her best friend Sophie.

JEN: Ah.

TILLY: There's this German girl in my year, Hannah, she used to be a boy called Hans.

JEN: No, I draw the line at that. Fifteen year olds getting sex change operations?

TILLY: No operation. Just identifies as female.

JEN: Oh yeah, clever parents to get little Hans into the best girls' school in London!

TILLY: Mum that is just heartless!

JEN: No, come on, I can't believe the school governors allowed that.

TILLY: Oh, you'd rather let Hannah be bullied to death in a boy's school for wearing dresses and makeup? I thought you were a better human than that.

JEN: No, wait, I am. I'm sorry. It just seems to me that maybe your friends might be a little … confused. Or going through a phase. Experimenting. Which is natural at this age. For some. I didn't.

TILLY: They are expressing their freedom to be whomever they want.

JEN: Good use of whomever.

TILLY: We are campaigning to do away with the gender binary system.

JEN: Sorry?

TILLY: Men and women. The heterosexual norm. Leaves out a whole host of other possibilities.

JEN: You mean gay people?

TILLY: LGBT just isn't enough anymore.

JEN: Lesbian, gay, bisexual and, and, don't tell me….

TILLY: Trans, Mum, come on. But now there's Q.

JEN: Quick?

TILLY: Questioning! Gender fluid … And then there's Blake.

JEN: What's a Blake?

TILLY: They don't identify as male or female. They don't want to be assigned a sex.

JEN: So these people who are asexual are called Blakes?

TILLY: No, not asexual, that means someone who isn't interested in sex. Blake's definitely interested in sex.

JEN: How on earth did they come up with the name Blake as a category of sexual preference?

TILLY: Gender identity. No, it's Blake's name. They don't want to be identified as male or female, just as a person.

JEN: Ah okay, I think I saw this in *Star Trek* once. But I still don't understand how many Blakes there are?

TILLY: What?

JEN: You keep saying they.

TILLY: They. As in not he or she. Gender neutral.

JEN: Blake is one person?

TILLY: Yes. Blake is a person I know, a friend, and they want to be known as they!

JEN: That can't be right. They is plural.

TILLY: Is it? You said they when you talked about the school.

JEN: I meant they who run the school, not the building or concept of a school. You are talking about a human being.

TILLY: Argh!!!

JEN: Show me a picture.

TILLY: What?

JEN: Of Blake. Surely if this person is a friend of yours you have a picture of them on Facebook.

TILLY: You said them!

JEN: Oh God, there must be a better pronoun. Like the French use "on" for one. Impersonal.

Tilly shows Jen her phone.

TILLY: There, that's Blake.

JEN: That's Justin Bieber.

TILLY: What?

JEN: You remember how in love you were with Justin Bieber? That's who she looks like.

TILLY: Mum! That is horrible!

JEN: What?

TILLY: You in your stupid cisgender world, you'll never understand!

JEN: Cis–?

TILLY: Cisgender. Identifying with the gender you're born with.

JEN: But that's normal right? Is that a bad thing now?

TILLY: No! It's neither good nor bad. There shouldn't be any normal! That's what we're campaigning for. (She notices something on her phone) Oh what?

JEN: What is it?

TILLY: Nothing. I can't believe it.

Tilly starts searching Facebook on her laptop and then texting on her phone.

JEN: What?

Tilly gets a text back which she reads and then texts a reply while talking.

TILLY: This is just … hang on. (Her phone rings) Sophie, you okay? … When? Yeah, no, I mean, of course, you must be gutted. Are you sure? … She broke up with you? (Looks at laptop again) oh my God, you're right. Let me check their status … no, they didn't change it. So wait, you only found out 'cos Alexa changed her status? That is not on … no, that really isn't…. Okay, okay, call me when you hear anything. I'm sorry, babe, really. Bye.

Tilly has tears in her eyes as she hangs up her phone.

JEN: Everything okay?

TILLY: Yeah, anyway, I'm uh … I've gotta go –

JEN: Sophie having relationship problems?

TILLY: Yeah, uh, Alexa cheated on her. Last week, but she only found out. But like, I guess, you know, it's not like they're married or anything.

JEN: With Blake?

TILLY: What? No. What do you mean?

JEN: You were on Blake's Facebook page. (Beat) Oh God.

TILLY: What?

JEN: You're in love with Blake.

TILLY: No!

JEN: Tilly, it's okay, I'm not judging. I'm trying really hard to understand –

TILLY: You don't know anything! I don't love … anyone –

JEN: But I'm guessing Blake doesn't feel the same?

TILLY: I don't want to talk about it.

JEN: Sweetie, we talk about everything!

TILLY: You don't have to know everything about me. I'm allowed a private life, aren't I? Maybe there are some things I can never tell you because we are two very different people. (She gets a phone notification) What?? No!!

JEN: Oh dear.

TILLY: Oh my God. (Searches through her phone) No, this is unreal. (She dials phone, gets up and walks away from Jen) Jess, is it true? But he's like in a totally different group. He goes out with like popular girls. You actually saw them together … what party? Oh, no, I wasn't invited, I don't hang out with him normally … yeah, so somebody posted a picture … yeah, they did. I don't get it … no, we're just friends. (Tearing up again) I'm just … okay, laters.

Tilly hangs up her phone. As Jen puts her arms around her she bursts into tears.

JEN: What happened?

TILLY: It's just not fair! I was there for her, them, and being really supportive and then it's like no, she's too, I mean, they's too, argh! They're too good for me now, and like in a whole other group of people, who are like way cooler than me, 'cos like I look like so fucking heteronormative and –

JEN: Whoa, whoa, slow down. She who?

TILLY: Blake! Blake is just really cool and writes poetry and goes on marches and doesn't give two fucks about anything and –

JEN: Language!

TILLY: Sorry. She … I mean they used to be Carrie and really shy and got bullied a lot and then became Blake and now everyone wants to be with them. But only after I became friends with her. Them. And I thought we had a thing, I don't know. I've never had a boyfriend and I thought maybe I prefer girls but I don't because I've never been attracted to any girl like I have to Blake.

JEN: Who looks a lot like –

TILLY: Fucking Justin Bieber!/

JEN: /A boy. Language! Okay, so Blake and you …?

TILLY: I thought we were together, okay? I … didn't tell anyone because I thought no one would understand, not my close friends anyway. I mean they're all cool with destroying the patriarchy and doing away with gender binary systems and all but they just wouldn't expect it of me especially after Belinda's party when I got off with George de Wilde, but that was only because I'd always had a crush on him from like year five and –

JEN: Got off?

TILLY: Oh just forget it!

Tilly pulls away.

JEN: No, stay, come on …

TILLY: So … so then Carrie becomes Blake and I'm like more confused than ever and there is no one I can talk to except Alexa Lucas 'cos at least she's dating Sophie but even she thinks Blake is just a lesbian but won't commit. And then … and then … Blake gets off with Alexa!

JEN: Oh, right, that's not nice.

TILLY: I know! So then Alexa breaks up with Sophie 'cos she thinks Blake is into her. And Sophie is like, "what the fuck?" She's in pieces.

JEN: Oh dear.

TILLY: And then, then, who do you think Blake decides they're in love with?

JEN: Sophie?

TILLY: George de Wilde!

JEN: I can't keep up with this.

TILLY: Yeah, so basically Blake wants to get off with anyone in the world except me.

JEN: When you say get off, do you mean....

TILLY: Why not me? What's wrong with me?

JEN: No, don't you dare. There is nothing wrong with you, Tilly. You are beautiful and bright and deserve someone who loves you completely for who you are. And you are only ... fifteen. Fifteen!

TILLY: But I don't know who I am.

JEN: You are Tilly. And you are funny and sarcastic and clever. And maybe Blake doesn't know who ... they are. At fifteen. And just really needed you to be a supportive friend.

TILLY: Oh ... yeah. A friend.

JEN: Friendship is sometimes the most important thing of all.

TILLY: Or maybe Blake is just a complete bitch!

JEN: Uh-uh, that's not gender fluid.

TILLY: Oh ... right. I didn't mean it. It just ... wait, are you taking the piss?

JEN: No.

TILLY: I mean I was so into this fight for equality and then Blake has to just go and ruin everything.

JEN: No, you need to keep campaigning. Fight for what you believe. I think it's great that your generation is so open-minded.

TILLY: You do?

JEN: Yes, I mean I've always had lots of gay friends, but I have to admit I used to think bisexual people were just greedy.

TILLY: Mum! You're being horrible again.

JEN: So it's good for me to learn about this, what a ... spectrum there is of sexuality.

TILLY: Yeah. So you're not totally grossed out by me being into Blake?

JEN: Well, it's just a different side to you that I didn't know about, I guess.

TILLY: You are grossed out.

JEN: I just have to get used to it.

TILLY: Okay.

JEN: It just seems to me –

TILLY: Here we go.

JEN: No, hear me out. Aren't you actually putting even more labels on people instead of just letting them figure out who they are? I mean, you're all growing up and constantly changing. So these labels and letters might just change from day to day. Q one day, L the next, who knows?

TILLY: Maybe. But it's better to know that there are other people like you and that you're not some freak of nature.

JEN: Androgynous! That's the word I was looking for. Like David Bowie used to be.

TILLY: Did you fancy him?

JEN: Of course, everyone did. But he was –

TILLY: A man?

JEN: I was going to say … David Bowie. Anyway, maybe the best thing to do is just stay out of all this mess for a while and focus on, I don't know, school?

TILLY: You mean be celibate?

JEN: Not for the rest of your life, just until you're a little older.

TILLY: And miss out on those orgasms? No way!

JEN: I … oh, you're joking.

TILLY: Maybe.

JEN: Or … tell Blake how you feel.

TILLY: Why? She's with George de Wilde now and like put it on Instagram so….

JEN: So, she's a she now that they're with George de Wilde?

TILLY: Oh, no. I don't know.

JEN: Look, Blake is a friend of yours, who treated you really badly.

TILLY: Blake has a right to –

JEN: Hurt other people by … by getting off with two of your friends?

TILLY: Maybe I misunderstood our … relationship.

JEN: Doesn't give Blake the right to be shitty.

TILLY: Mum! Language. Anyway, nothing major ever … happened between me and Blake so –

JEN: Blake and I. (Beat) So when you say nothing major –

TILLY: Can we finish my essay? It was due yesterday.

JEN: Yesterday? Why didn't you-? (Tilly gives her a "don't you dare" look) Okay, okay. Never mind. (Pause. She goes back to laptop, looking at essay.) Hey! Look on the bright side. At least Blake didn't get you pregnant.

Tilly shakes her head, closes laptop, picks it up and walks away in silence.

JEN: Tilly, honey, I'm kidding, really … sort of.

Ends.

Afterword

Lydia Parker

A Better Pronoun grew out of conversations I had with my daughter when she was a teenager. It seemed to me at the time that her friends were constantly changing their sexual preferences as well as the objects of their crushes, and not only was I confused but I concluded they must be as well. My daughter was very patient with me and explained to me over and over the many permutations of sexuality and gender in this brave new world. Having grown up in New York City I'd thought I was the most open-minded and sophisticated person one could meet. I was wrong. It took me a while but I eventually grew to understand and appreciate that young people are demanding the freedom to be who they are inside, all of the time. It takes courage and I truly believe everyone in the world should have that freedom. I'm so proud of my daughter's generation because the movement is spreading to the older generation and to other groups who feel "different". Acceptance is a beautiful thing. But I still think we need a better pronoun.

Part VII
The class ceiling

19　*The Pillory*

Felix O'Brien

Characters

FLICK, *early twenties, white, upper class.*
LAUREN, *early twenties, any race, working class.*

Notes

(/) indicates a point of interruption.
(–) at the end of a line indicates being cut off.
(…) indicates where speech trails off.
(/) indicates the point where the immediately following dialogue interrupts.
(Silence) indicates the point at which characters do not know what to say next or how to say it.
(Pause) indicates where there is a thought process happening.

Original production details

The Pillory was commissioned by Little Pieces of Gold for the 'Class Ceiling' Festival which was produced at the Bread and Roses Theatre on 17 to 18 April 2016 and at the Southwark Playhouse on 20 March 2016.

The cast was as follows:

LAUREN	Georgia Nicholson
FLICK	Rebecca Rayne
Director:	Hannah Jones

Police cells. Winter. Late. Flick, dressed for a night out, paces, trying to keep herself warm. Lauren, dressed more casually, is still. Neither of them has shoes on.

Silence.

FLICK:　Bloody cold in here.

Pause.

No?

LAUREN: Mm.

FLICK: Can't believe they took my jacket.

LAUREN: Standard. They have to.

FLICK: Don't see why. Bloody ridiculous! No pockets in the thing. And they'd already bloody searched me! Thoroughly. Not like there's any way I could've I could've/smuggled –

LAUREN: It's in case you hang yourself.

Pause.

FLICK: Does that actually happen? That doesn't actually happen.

LAUREN: Not when they take your jacket off you. And your belt. Laces, etcetera. Covering their arses.

FLICK: Right.

Pause.

I'm Felicity, by the way. Flick.

Pause.

And you are?

LAUREN: Lauren.

FLICK: Should we hug, or –

LAUREN: No touching.

FLICK: Right. Yeah … It's actually alright in here, really, isn't it? Expected worse, to be honest. Hear some real horror stories! But it's clean. Quiet. Just too bloody cold.

A lull.

They were lovely to me. At the desk thing. The sort of hairy little lady at the counter said she liked my dress. And one of the policemen was definitely looking at my bum. The sort of fit one. Which is super cheeky. But flattering.

LAUREN: It's a fucking disgrace! Fucking abuse of power, is what it is. Should be him in one of these. Fucking pervert.

FLICK: Don't be so dramatic. Men have eyes. They wander.

Lauren sneers. Flick scoffs.

FLICK: So. (Puts on a terrible American accent) "Whaddaya in for, then?"

LAUREN: Sorry, what?

Flick huffs.

FLICK: "Whaddaya in for, then?"
LAUREN: What are you doing?
FLICK: I'm being, like, a sort of gangster thing. Like, from Godfather or Sopranos or something.
LAUREN: Sound like Goofy.
FLICK: Do I? No I don't. I think it's quite good, actually.
LAUREN: It's not.
FLICK: No, it is.
LAUREN: Nah.
FLICK: (Tuts. She tries a slightly different accent) "Why is you up in this bitch, then, homie?"
LAUREN: That one's just fucking racist. Don't do that.
FLICK: Yeah, see, that time I was going for, like, Orange is the New Black?
LAUREN: More like White is the Daft Cunt.

Flick is aghast.

FLICK: Sorry, who do/you think –
LAUREN: I was protesting.
FLICK: I gathered,/but –
LAUREN: No, I mean today. I was protesting. That's "what I'm in for". To answer your ... question.
FLICK: Right.
LAUREN: Aye. Me and a couple of mates from Uni. Was brilliant. Worth it.
FLICK: What did you do?

Lauren smirks.

LAUREN: Covered ourselves in bacon and went to Number 10. Oinked a lot. Were there for a couple of minutes. Cops came. Might have been a bit mouthy. But I managed to shout "Osborne's a cokenosed prick" before they bunged us in the van. So I think we got the point across.
FLICK: Wow.
LAUREN: Felt a bit guilty. Just gone vegan, haven't I? But binning it all seemed like such a waste. And using it like that sent a message, you know? Proper did, like.

A lull.

FLICK: Revolutionary.
LAUREN: Aye, I know, right? Text my dad. Dead proud.
FLICK: Really?

LAUREN: Oh yeah! Course. Don't get me wrong, my mam was a bit "tsk tsk tsk". But my dad was chuffed to bits. Said he wished he could've joined us! Jezza's his screensaver. We've got posters of him in the window back home. The whole street does. Amazing.

FLICK: Sorry, who's "Jezza"?

LAUREN: Short for Jeremy.

FLICK: Kyle?

LAUREN: Corbyn.

FLICK: Got you.

Pause.

Is he like, a footballer,/or –

LAUREN: Fuck's sake! Jeremy Corbyn? Politician. Saviour of the/Labour Party.

FLICK: Ohhhhh! Oh, him, right. Scruffy man? From the news. A touch doddery? Looks a bit homeless?

LAUREN: Oi: that's The Future Prime Minister of Our Country you're on about.

FLICK: (Scoffs) Sure.

Silence. Lauren inhales.

LAUREN: So?

FLICK: What?

LAUREN: Your turn. Why are you in here?

FLICK: Oh. Right. Yeah.

Pause.

Bit embarrassing, actually.

LAUREN: Brilliant.

FLICK: I sort of might have punched someone in their face.

LAUREN: Serious?

FLICK: Hm. So naughty.

LAUREN: Who?

FLICK: (Sighs) I don't know.

LAUREN: What, was it just some random in the street?

FLICK: Oh, don't be ridiculous. As if I'd do something so … so tacky.

Pause.

It was in the bathroom. At Mahiki.

Lauren finds this hilarious.

It isn't bloody funny! It's mortifying. I'm so embarrassed.

LAUREN: Oh my God, this is class. So what happened?

FLICK: Well ... I mean, it was extortion, really.

LAUREN: Extortion?

FLICK: I'd just been out for a cigarette. I don't smoke. Only when I've been drinking. And I'd been talking to this super-hot guy. Looked a bit tatty and Dalstonish, but he was wearing Aventus so he's on at least 40k. Sneaky City Boy, as it turns out. Result! Freddie. Ugh. Gorgeous. And he smelled amazing and I smelled like Guy Fawkes so I went off to freshen up. In the Ladies'. Used some of their awful cheap deodorant stuff.... Had a few bits of chewing gum or whatever. And then this bloody attendant started getting all aggy and demanding money! And I told her I only had my AmEx, which was true – I mean, like, who even carries cash? Like, nobody, right?

Pause.

Right. Exactly. So I tried to placate her but her English was abysmal. Like, sub-GCSE. And basically it became this whole big misunderstanding and one thing led to another and basically, long story short, I punched her a bit. Only twice. Wait:

Pause.

No. Three times. And the police came. And I did have a ring on which made it look worse than it was. Only a costume piece, but ... sturdy. And now I'm here. Freezing.

Pause.

Hope Freddie didn't see. Scuffed knuckles are so not a good look. But I do smell a bit better, actually. So....

Flick weighs the two things up.

Swings and roundabouts, really.

LAUREN: Oh my God, you're Cheryl fucking Cole! The Nation's Sweetheart!

FLICK: Oh, don't say that! As if I'm her.

Shudders.

Honestly I feel awful. Daddy would be mortified.

LAUREN: "Daddy".

FLICK: I'm never drinking again. Honestly. Can't believe I'd do something so so so ... so ... so chavvy.

Flick shudders. Lauren breathes.

LAUREN: Meaning?

FLICK: Hm? Oh, nothing. Just, y'know. Bit.... Bit common, isn't it?

LAUREN: What?

FLICK: What?

LAUREN: Common?

FLICK: Yeah. Sorry, have I said something/wrong?

LAUREN: Yeah, you have, actually. You really have. Fucking posh twat.

FLICK: Excuse me?

LAUREN: Want me to say it louder? FUCKING. POSH./TWAT.

FLICK: Oh, shut up, for God's sake. You're embarrassing yourself. Have a bit of decorum.

LAUREN: "Decorum"? Fuck's/sake.

FLICK: Yes. Decorum. It means/class.

LAUREN: I know what – Jesus Christ. I swear, if this was anywhere else,/I'd –

FLICK: Oh, a threat? Lovely. Well, it isn't anywhere else, is it? It's here. Ha. And may I remind you that I very recently won my first fight? So I'm actually on a bit of a roll.

Lauren laughs.

LAUREN: Punching an immigrant in the head doesn't/count as –

FLICK: Who said she was an immigrant?

Silence.

She called me a slut. Yeah! Under her breath, but I heard it. "Stupid white slut", she said. So she's not some blameless bloody Oxfam poster you have up in your little common room. Get that out of your head. She's the racist, if/anything.

LAUREN: This is hell. I must be in hell. I've actually died and gone to hell. Swear I could smell drink on the policeman's breath. Squad car must have fucking Princess Died/or something.

FLICK: Don't you dare bring her into this.

LAUREN: And now I've fucking actually died. And I'm stuck in fucking limbo with Lady Colin fucking Campbell.

FLICK: That is a horrible thing to say.

Pause.

She lives in Kennington.

Flick gags. Lauren seethes.

Oh, come on! That was a joke! Obviously that was a joke. Lighten up. You're being ridiculous.

LAUREN: Can you just ... not talk anymore? Doing my head in.

FLICK: Honestly, I try to be nice. Make conversation. Crack a few/jokes –
LAUREN: Still talking!
FLICK: Do not interrupt me. Don't ever interrupt me.

Pause.

I can't bear rudeness. Not how I was raised.
LAUREN: Fuck me!
FLICK: You swear too much.
LAUREN: What, were you not raised that way?
FLICK: No. Of course not. I've never heard my parents swear.
LAUREN: Must not need to.
FLICK: No one needs to. It's just fun.
LAUREN: No, people do. People do.

Flick tuts.

My dad's been made redundant three times. Outlasted every job he's ever had.
   Lumber yard. Textiles. Semiconductors. Now he mops floors and cleans
   toilets for six fifty an hour.
FLICK: Oh, come on! That's not bad at all!
LAUREN: Are you fucking –

Pause.

Six pounds fifty.
FLICK: Oh. Hm. Wow.
LAUREN: No: "Jesus. Fuck. Shit." That's what you mean.
FLICK: No, no, I get it. That's hard. That must be hard. Sorry.

Pause.

My sister's a doctor. Emily.
LAUREN: Course she fucking is.
FLICK: She said, when you break it down, pro rata, she'd make about the same
   working in Aldi. I mean … Aldi. Not even, one of the good ones.
LAUREN: My mum works in Aldi.

Flick groans.

FLICK: Well, d'you know what? Lucky her. Seven years of hardcore Uni and
   Emily comes to ours to eat out of the fridge. Lives off pitta and dip. Still
   can't make her rent. Well, I mean, who can, but still…. Ridiculous.
LAUREN: Bet you're regretting voting Tory now, eh?
FLICK: I didn't vote Tory. Didn't vote at all. I was in Mauritius.

Lauren kicks something. Really hurts herself.

You alright?
LAUREN: Fucking hurts.
FLICK: Forgot you didn't have your Docs on?
LAUREN: How did you know I/had –
FLICK: Come on. Come on. Of course you wear Docs. Because they'd go per-
   fectly with the parka you were definitely wearing.

Pause.

Eh?
LAUREN: It was a Harrington, actually.
FLICK: I stand corrected.

Pause. Lauren shivers.

Cold?
LAUREN: Course I fucking am.
FLICK: Hm. Supposed to snow tonight.
LAUREN: Fuck.
FLICK: Yeah.

Pause.

LAUREN: Could be worse.
FLICK: How?
LAUREN: We're inside, at least. Roof over our heads. Even if it's not our
   own roof.
FLICK: Hm.
LAUREN: Some people don't.
FLICK: I suppose.
LAUREN: Somewhere.
FLICK: In the world.
LAUREN: In London, even.
FLICK: Yeah.
LAUREN: Round the corner. Outside Tescos. Sleeping on spikes.

Pause.

It's a big fucking issue.

Lauren laughs.

Didn't even mean that, then.

FLICK: Mean what?
LAUREN: "Big Issue". You know, like the ... the magazine?

Flick doesn't.

Never mind.

Silence.

FLICK: Wow. Some people don't get a roof.
LAUREN: What?
FLICK: It's literally only just occurred to me. I mean, I know people are worse-off. I get that. That's fine.
LAUREN: Fine?
FLICK: Not fine, no, obviously not fine. But I get that. I understand that. There are, y'know: (Indicates "levels")
But I suppose I've never actually realised that some people don't even get to have a roof. Like ... realised realised. No roof. Even when it snows.
LAUREN: Yeah. I know.

Pause.

Shit, isn't it?
FLICK: Yeah.

Silence.

Jesus.

Pause.

Fuck.

Silence.

I want to go home now.
LAUREN: Aye. Well tough tits, pet. You're here for the night. Make yourself/comfy.
FLICK: What? Oh, right. No, I'm not staying. Sorry!
LAUREN: "Night in the cells" usually lasts a night.
FLICK: Oh, right, yes. Yeah, I can see how you thought that. Sorry, should've said. My uncle Michael's sending a car for me.
LAUREN: Well, I hope the driver's brought a book to read/or something.
FLICK: Michael Gove.

Pause.

He's the Minister for –
LAUREN: I know who he is.
FLICK: Yes.

Pause.

I'm only here til the car comes. He's promised not to tell Daddy. Said "these
things happen, darling. Don't let it upset you." He's a good man.
LAUREN: You look nothing like him.
FLICK: I know. I look like Mummy.

Pause.

Thank God.
LAUREN: This is fucked. I do a bit of political oinking and get banged up. You
make a woman bleed and walk free. Just because of who your uncle is. It's
fucked, man. The world is just....

Lauren exhales heavily. Pause.

FLICK: Not my fault. I didn't make the world. Just live in it.

Ends.

Afterword

Felix O'Brien

In 2016, I was asked by Suzette Coon, Artistic Director of Little Pieces of Gold,
to contribute to an event called "The Class Ceiling", in which several writers
would respond to existing plays that had class as a primary theme. I chose to
respond to Laura Wade's brilliant play *Posh*, and *The Pillory* was the result. I
aimed to explore how wealth and influence affect how we view the world and
how the world views us. It's a study in contrasts: rich/poor, political/apolitical,
Southern/unSouthern. It's about trying to find common ground in a society that
seeks to stratify and divide us. It's about justice. It's about violence. It's about
power.

There are also jokes. And swearing. And sweary jokes. I chose to write an all-
female piece, as I didn't want to write another privileged man into existence.
We've got plenty. The piece was brilliantly directed by Hannah Jones and played
with wit and intelligence by Georgia Nicholson (Lauren) and Rebecca Rayne
(Flick). I was very happy with the response to the piece and I'm delighted to be
able to share it with you in print.

However, revisiting this piece in 2019 to write this (literal) postscript has
proven surprisingly bittersweet. I initially intended to update the references to

the 2016 political and social landscape (Corbyn, Gove, Lady Colin Campbell – who had a brief spell of jungle-based notoriety the previous winter), but found that I couldn't do so without rendering the original play entirely unrecognisable. Too much has changed too quickly. This play was staged prior to the Brexit vote and, as such, seems almost ludicrously naive now. Then, it was feasible to imagine some bacon-clad students being arrested for "political oinking". Now, packs of men in hi-vis vests openly abuse politicians and commentators at their place of work with little fear of real reprisal. Debate is debased. Our landscape has changed. We've skidded face-first into a darker timeline. With a boot firmly planted on the back of our neck. The play still works, but only as a period piece. It's cynical. But it's not 2019 cynical.

I couldn't write this play now. I'm too angry. Disillusioned. Disgusted by what this country has become. Hopefully, by the time this book reaches your hands, things will have changed for the better. I would love that to be the case.

Thank you for reading.

Felix O'Brien, January 2019

20 *Tussy*

Jaki McCarrick

Characters

WILL THORNE, *31, a gas worker at Beckton Gas Works.*
ELEANOR MARX, *33, an agitator and labour activist.*

Notes

(/) denotes the point of interruption in overlapping dialogue.
(…) denotes where speech trails off.
(Beat) denotes a brief break in the dialogue.
Words in square brackets are not to be spoken.

Original production details

Tussy was commissioned by Little Pieces of Gold for the "Class Ceiling"
Festival which was produced at the Bread and Roses Theatre on 17 to 18 April
2016 and at the Southwark Playhouse on 20 March 2016.

The cast was as follows:

ELEANOR MARX	Jess Murphy
WILL THORNE	Mike Corsale
Director:	Sharon Willems

Scene One

Hyde Park, London, 1888. Workers are gathered to listen to a number of speak-
ers. Will Thorne, a gas worker at Beckton Gas Works, has already spoken. (Will
is making a name for himself as an agitator.) Now, Eleanor Marx speaks. She
stands on a chair so she can be heard and seen by the crowd. It's a warm day so
her cloak is flung off, her sleeves uncuffed and rolled up. Behind her – a row of
seats where the previous and subsequent speakers wait. On one of these, stage-
right, sits Will Thorne. He nods approvingly throughout Eleanor's speech and
listens carefully. She draws to a close.

ELEANOR: I am speaking this afternoon not only as a trade unionist, but as a socialist. Socialists believe that the eight hours day is the first and most immediate step to be taken, and we aim at a time when there will be no longer one class supporting two others, but the unemployed both at the bottom – and at the top – of society will be got rid of. This is not the end but only the beginning of the struggle; it is not enough to come here to demonstrate in favour of an eight hours' day. We must not be like some Christians who sin for six days and go to church on the seventh, but we must speak for the cause daily, and make the men – and especially the women – that we meet, come into the ranks to help us. In conclusion, I would like to quote from a poem by Shelley – who else you might say (jokingly; Will laughs) – from his invocation to working class men – and women – the world over. From The Masque of Anarchy: "Rise like Lions after slumber.... In unvanquishable number, Shake your chains to earth like dew.... Which in a sleep had fallen on you – Ye are many – they are few." (Much of this speech is quoted from Eleanor Marx's actual speeches and essays written around this time.)

The crowd applauds and shouts up support. Will Thorne stands and gestures to Eleanor to a free seat beside him. She sits. The next speaker gets up from the row of seats to speak (this we do not see) and readies himself for the chair-slash-podium. The following conversation is quiet, less animated, etc., as it is in full view of the public, and as the next speaker is readying himself, etc.

WILL: They liked that.
ELEANOR: I do hope so.
WILL: Will. Will Thorne.

He sticks out his hand, Eleanor shakes it, firmly.

ELEANOR: I know. I think you know my [husband] ... Edward? (She gestures further down the row) I'm Eleanor Marx.

Will nods.

WILL: Ben's up next. Poor sod. Doesn't rouse them like you. Old stoker they call you, now I know why.
ELEANOR: They call me what, sorry?

Beat.

WILL: Don't tell me you didn't know. *Our* old stoker, to be precise. A term of endearment, I suppose.
ELEANOR: It's not the stoker bit that bothers me.

Beat.

WILL: Mother always told me 'bout shooting my mouth off. (Beat) God. Look at him. He'll find those papers soon enough. Good egg though. Very precise. Likes to read the exact thing he's written. One. Word. At a time. (Shouts over at the speaker) G'wan Ben, go for it! You tell 'em, my man. That's it.

Beat.

ELEANOR: Your speech was absolutely riveting.
WILL: You havin' me on or what?
ELEANOR: No. You spoke from the heart. And you can think on your feet, too. I've never seen anything like it. No notes – or papers. Even George Bernard Shaw read from his papers.

A loud clap from the crowd for the point the current speaker, Ben Tillet, has just made. Will and Eleanor follow suit; they nod and clap.

WILL: Can't claim any credit for that I'm afraid, Miss.
ELEANOR: Eleanor.
WILL: Eleanor. Let's just say, it's true what they say: necessity is the mother of invention.
ELEANOR: What do you/mean?
WILL: Oh – it's nought.

Eleanor looks at Will, intuits what he means....

ELEANOR: Are you – are you saying – that you (whispers) can't actually read?
WILL: Aye. I can't. Not rightly anyway.

Beat.

ELEANOR: Well, we shall just have to do something about that.
WILL: Ya see, I've not had time to learn. And it's my brain – the words jump about the page.
ELEANOR: William Thorne, now that I know your little secret, there's not a chance in hell I'm letting you continue as you are.

Fade lights.

Scene Two

Eleanor Marx's living room, Bloomsbury, 1888. She is at her desk, typing. In the room there is a chez longue with lots of books piled up on it; books, too, on the surfaces of the furniture and all around the floor. The window is open, the voile curtains move lightly in the summer breeze. Eleanor hears footsteps outside and goes to the window – which looks to the street. She peers out.

ELEANOR: It's alright Gerty. I'll get it.

Goes off to open the front door. We hear voices in the hallway – Eleanor's and Will Thorne's.

(OFF): How was – oh thank you, you shouldn't have.

Eleanor re-enters the room, followed by Will.

WILL: Got them in Silvertown. From one of the biscuit girls. There's shortbread in there and a new type. The jammy dodger they're calling it. Really nice they are.

Eleanor takes the tin of biscuits, places it on the table.

ELEANOR: You and I shall have them later. With tea.
WILL: Oh no – for yourself. Yourself – and Mr – Aveling....
ELEANOR: Edward. You must call him that. (Beat) Now. Sit. Please do.

Eleanor moves some books off the chez longue and Will sits down, looks around, takes in the space. Eleanor regards him, observing his posture, which is poor – somewhat humped. Will reaches into his pocket, counts out change in his hand.

WILL: Could you tell me – Eleanor – how much you might charge?
ELEANOR: I beg your pardon?
WILL: For the lessons. I'd like to be straight with you from the off. If you don't mind.
ELEANOR: Oh please, Mr Thorne. Will. I am not going to charge you a farthing. This is for the cause, don't you see that?

Will puts his money away, embarrassed.

You're going to lead the Beckton gas workers in a union one day. If anyone can get the eight hours day it will be you, Sir. You are the man for the job. No doubt in my mind about it. So I see it as my duty to get you ready for that eventuality.

Beat.

WILL: How can you be so sure? I'm just a hired hand – like everyone else at the works. I don't have a contract. I vie for work with the best of 'em.
ELEANOR: That speech you gave in the Park. I still think about it. People were crying, did you know that? That's a gift, Will. A rare one. You didn't even use notes. Of course, now – I know why.

Will looks away, a mixture of embarrassment and pride from her praise.

ELEANOR: Tell me about yourself.

Beat.

WILL: Well, I'm a grafter. Working since I was six. Four miles to the job, there and back. Saw my mother and sisters graft themselves to the bone, sewing hooks and eyes into cards. Broken my back – literally in places – up here and here – due to carrying weighty bags before I was twelve. The lot of the labour classes? I've lived it. Seen the worst of it. Came up from Birmingham four years ago only to find London worse. Factory workers of Silvertown working themselves stupid while the rich get richer off of it.
ELEANOR: "Off" it – not "off of".

Will looks confused.

What I mean to say, "off of" sounds.... Look, never mind. We'll come back to it. Stand up will you?

Will stands.

Hmmm.
WILL: What is it?
ELEANOR: You know, I think I can see that back issue. Try and straighten up – can you do that? That's it.
WILL: You sound like my mother.
ELEANOR: Has to be better than "old stoker", eh?
WILL: Can't believe I told you that. My big mouth. Just can't keep it shut.
ELEANOR: Well that's a good trait in this house, Will. Breathe in, will you? (He does) What happens to you when you read? Can you make the words out? I mean, you must be able to read something – that speech you gave was full of cadences that one could only have acquired from reading, surely?
WILL: The words jump when I read. I do see 'em – but they jump. That's the only way I can describe it. They go back the front sort of.
ELEANOR: I see. Pick up that book. What does it say on the cover?
WILL: "Mad – am – Vo" – sorry, no – "Bo – vary. Pro vin – vin – vinical"– (he stops, frustrated).
ELEANOR: Breathe.

Will breathes, relaxes, reads.

WILL: "Provincial Manners."
ELEANOR: That's it, exactly. You know, I think I've read about your condition before –

WILL: Aye, it's called being bloody illiterate.

ELEANOR: No – no it's to do with the eye, and not breathing properly, and being tense. And I've heard that reading on coloured paper helps. It's something we'll look into as we go along. Though I'm not a doctor.

WILL: What's it about?

ELEANOR: What?

WILL: This. (The book)

ELEANOR: Oh. It's about a woman trapped in a marriage – well, more "buried" than trapped – who eventually kills herself. I've just translated it for George Moore. Take that copy home with you, I've loads.

WILL: Some sort of brute is he, her husband?

ELEANOR: No – he's completely average in every way. And in his world Emma Bovary is incapable of realising herself. Not unlike the workers of Silvertown, really – though Emma is much less aware than they. Emma's the real star of the piece only she doesn't know it of course. It's really a very wonderful book. Flaubert doesn't pretty anything up, and for that he was lambasted. It's a book about boredom in many ways, too – and who has the balls to write about that nowadays? Something so real. And so deadly. Nobody – apart from Mr Ibsen perhaps.

Beat.

WILL: Translate a lot of these kind of books do you?

ELEANOR: No. (She smiles)

Will nods, looks around – pictures of Karl Marx and his books are everywhere. He sees a framed picture of Karl Marx with some writing scrawled across it.

WILL: "To Tuss-Tuss-…"

ELEANOR: (Corrects his pronunciation) Tussy. As in pussycat. Not as in fussy. It's my nickname. I would call him the "Mohr" and he would call me Tussy. Maybe because I love cats. I can't remember exactly. You may call me Tussy if you wish, all my friends do.

Slight beat.

WILL: I prefer Eleanor. (Beat) So is this – where you all … [were reared]?

ELEANOR: Oh no. That was Soho. Then Kentish Town.

WILL: It's nice. Here.

ELEANOR: Thank you. It can get cold. (Pause) When we've got you reading, Will – you'll be able to quote from any one of these books. For your speeches. Quotes give a speech power. Then maybe you'll be able to teach.

WILL: Steady on! (Beat) Ya know, the match girls – the biscuit girls – everyone in Silvertown in fact – they adore you. Now, I know why. (He's said too much again) What I mean is – you genuinely care – about others. It's like you're putting into practice – his (indicates to the picture) – ideas. They'd just be that – ideas – if it weren't for you.

ELEANOR: And Edward of course.

Will nods, closes the book. Straightens his back.

WILL: Where is he now then – Mr Aveling?

ELEANOR: At his club. The theatre perhaps. (Beat.) So. Let's get to work. I need to think what to do about your posture. While you, Will, just need to get quiet – breathe – and read. And then we shall have some of your biscuits.

Fade lights.

Scene Three

Some weeks later. Same setting as before. It's now autumn, October-ish – and the room is colder. Eleanor and Will wear warmer clothes – cardigans, etc. Eleanor seems distraught but is masking it. Will is reading from Madame Bovary, straight-backed, taking in deep breaths, reaching for a deep register in his voice; he is a great orator.

WILL: (Reading from Madame Bovary) "Stop it! She cried out with a terrible look. And rushing from the parlour, Emma slammed the door so hard that the bar – the baro ..." (Will struggles here) –

ELEANOR: "Barometer ..."

WILL: "the barometer jumped off the wall and smashed on the floor."

Eleanor nods. Will detects something is wrong with her. Decides to give her his news now.

WILL: I've been working on a plan.

ELEANOR: Plan?

WILL: Yes. A union.

ELEANOR: ?

WILL: A union, Eleanor. At the gasworks. Followed by negotiations for an eight hour day. Then when we don't get that, I'm going to call a strike. In winter. Latest – February or March. Just when they need us most.

Beat.

ELEANOR: Oh – that's/wonderful.

WILL: I'd like you to organise it with me. Whole thing. Speak to the men – and their wives. They need to stick together. No divide and rule this time. They will listen to you.

ELEANOR: But of course.

WILL: My speeches though – I'm worried they'll be … I'm worried if the bosses find out how pig-shit thick I am.…

ELEANOR: You are not thick. Your reading has improved beyond measure. You'll be writing fluently by spring, I'll make sure of it. Oh, but this is great news, Will. I'll help. Paperwork, newsletters. And you'll need rules and accounts. These bosses are slippery, believe me; they will try to trip you up. This is what we hoped would happen. Crank it up at the gasworks – then hit them over the head with a dockers' strike. It's wonderful. Edward and I will write about it when the time comes. We often work as a team, as you know – and he can organise with us, he's an actor – a natural on the stage, as you saw yourself at Hyde Park … (Beat) What – what is it – what have I said?

WILL: Eleanor for Christ's sake.…

ELEANOR: What?

WILL: Aveling. (Long beat) Why can't you see it? Everyone in the SDF knows.

ELEANOR: Knows what?

WILL: For one who values truth so much you (Beat) Edward Aveling is a liability. A cad. And more. Alright then. I've said it./

ELEANOR: Will … how … how dare you!/

WILL: No, I've not said it! I've not said it at all. He – Aveling – he fucks everything that moves and spends your money doing it – while you're out there – changing lives. Changing London. You can do so much better, Eleanor. And he – your precious Edward – is borrowing – no not borrowing – he's fucking stealing the light from your star. There. Big mouth strikes again. (Beat) Look/I.…

ELEANOR: Stop. Right. There.

WILL: I'm sorry.… But I just can't understand how such a brilliant woman could…

ELEANOR: Could what?

WILL: Love such a … (Pause) Actually. Maybe I do.

ELEANOR: You do what?

WILL: Understand. (Beat – as if trying to explain his previous outburst) Ya see, I was brought up by women. My father died in a fight when I was seven. My mother worked. So I'm used to – a – a matriarchy, I suppose. It's my habit. I'm lucky my habit then matches my words. But you – your words are all for equality but your habit is to serve a man. First him – Karl – and now Aveling. Even me in a way. You know equality intellectually – but somehow not – emotionally. In here – deep in your heart – you Eleanor Marx – the most brilliant woman I know, possibly the most brilliant woman alive on the planet today – and you can't see your own power. That's why I refuse to call you Tussy. It's a small name for a great woman. So, I then begin to be afraid for the women in the factories – the biscuit girls, the match girls – for their lives in the home – for if you – like bloody Emma Bovary – are not free at the taproot of it all – how can they be?

Will goes to put his jacket on, gather his things.

I'll leave now shall I?

ELEANOR: No. No don't.

Long uncomfortable silence.

WILL: (Shivering) Right about this house. It is cold.

ELEANOR: It's called dyslexia. The words jumping around the page thing.

Will nods.

WILL: You were upset today from the off. And I think I know why. Because I know where he is, and you know where he is, too.

ELEANOR: It's no one's business but ours.

WILL: You're right. I'm sorry. I spoke out of turn./I'll go.

Beat.

ELEANOR: Have you ever – ever had a broken heart, Will?

WILL: Course.

He feels as if he would like to go to her – but this is a friendship.

ELEANOR: Sometimes it gives you clarity. (Pause) You've hit on something true today. True that, the old bastard – the "system", the "patriarchy" – it's deep-rooted. It's in my marrow. Deeper than I thought.

WILL: It's in me, too. I'm no angel.

ELEANOR: (Paces the room, a "eureka" moment has arrived at exactly the worst time) Do you see, Will? Oh it's so clear to me now! The entire race is stunted – unless women are utterly free. The women question must come first. The whole dominance–submission paradigm? Change that and we change everything. Women, then the world. Not the other way round. You have the right to vote – I do not. That has to affect something inside me – and of every woman. In life, in affairs of the heart. You're absolutely right. But dear God – how do you go about changing human marrow – it will take years to change.

WILL: Aye. Perhaps centuries.

Ends.

Afterword

Jaki McCarrick

In 2011, while I was researching my play *Belfast Girls*, which quotes from Karl Marx's Communist Manifesto, I came across a reference to Marx's youngest daughter, Eleanor. The reference took the form of a footnote on a website about the history of the British Labour movement. I digressed from my research to find out more about this 'footnote'. Eleanor Marx intrigued me, as she seemed to be attempting to put into practice, in London, the ideas of her father – yet I had never heard of her. I decided to look for more information about her and when I came across the name of Eleanor Marx again in, of all things, an autobiography by Billy Bragg, I knew then that I would have to write something about her. I like to feel connections – and not just intellectually – with my subjects. I found this on several levels with Eleanor Marx. She had a love of the theatre (her partner, Edward Aveling, was an actor); she spoke out regularly about women's and workers' rights; she campaigned for Irish independence and would refer to herself as "Fenian Sister" in many of her letters. And I could particularly relate to her relationship with her father, a big personality, who considered his youngest daughter to be his political and intellectual heir. I had a similar intellectual bond with my own father. Later, I read Rachel Holmes' brilliant biography of Eleanor Marx, and Siobhan Brown's *A Rebel's Handbook*. I was interested in Marx's terrible end (she took her own life) and disastrous relationship with Edward Aveling, though I didn't want to be preoccupied with this. The aspect of that relationship which interests me most is how it represents a clear lag between her intellectual and emotional/psychological selves; the latter being very much governed, I consider, by the mores of the times. The relationship which most interests me in Marx's life was, and is still, also largely a footnote in her story, and that was with the trade unionist, Will Thorne. Thorne was a British trade unionist and activist from Birmingham who went on to achieve for workers the eight-hour day (which today we take very much for granted), and who was awarded a CBE in 1930. When Eleanor Marx first met Thorne he was illiterate, and she took it upon herself to teach Thorne reading and writing, and later introduced him to radical literature. Under her tutelage, Thorne went on to lead one of the most important strikes in the history of trade unionism, the 1889 Gas Workers' Strike. But history, until recently, had forgotten Marx's contribution to this important event. In *Tussy*, I explore the Marx/Thorne relationship as a 'way in' to the story of Eleanor Marx and her place in the history of the Labour movement, trade unionism, workers' rights, feminism, etc. After the Gas Workers' Strike, Thorne became a Member of Parliament and, until his death, attributed much of his success to his mentor.

Part VIII

Siblings in mourning

21 *Come Die With Me*

Vicki Connerty

Characters

RACHEL ROGERS, *late twenties.*
DAVID ROGERS, *early twenties, Rachel's brother.*
HELEN ROGERS, *mid-fifties, Rachel and David's mother.*

Notes

(–) at the end of a line indicates being cut off.
(…) at the end of a speech means it trails off. On its own it indicates a pressure or expectation to speak.
(Pause) indicates where there is a thought process happening.

Original production details

Come Die With Me was commissioned and produced by Little Pieces of Gold at Southwark Playhouse on 23 April 2017.

The cast was as follows:

RACHEL	Jess Murphy
HELEN	Alexis Leighton
DAVID	David Hopper
Director:	Sharon Willems

The living room of the Rogers family home. Rachel, Helen and David are squashed together uncomfortably on the small sofa, each holding a mug of tea. Directly in front of them a closed full-size coffin rests casually on a coffee table. In Helen's lap is a small pile of unopened envelopes. Occasionally the silence is broken by the sound of one of them awkwardly clearing their throat or drinking their tea. None of them take their eyes off the coffin. Eventually Rachel breaks the interminable silence.

RACHEL: I just think he would have been better off where he was.
HELEN: Yes, we know what you think, Rachel. But he's better off here.

Pause. They continue to observe the coffin.

DAVID: Just so you know, the lid's not screwed down.

RACHEL: What?!

HELEN: Why not?

DAVID: They said, "in case you want to take it off".

RACHEL: Why the fuck would we want to take the lid off?

HELEN: Rachel! Please. Language.

Helen gestures towards the coffin.

RACHEL: Sorry.

DAVID: Dunno. To say goodbye, I guess. The Irish do it, don't they? They get everyone round, hang out with the … (he points awkwardly at the coffin) for a few days, drink some Guinness, say goodbye. I think it's quite nice.

RACHEL: Good for them. We're not Irish. And that lid's staying put.

DAVID: Gran was born in Dublin actually. So that technically makes us a quarter Irish.

RACHEL: I don't care if Bono's my long lost uncle. We're not taking that lid off.

Pause.

HELEN: Did they say it was easy to get off, David?

RACHEL: Mum!

HELEN: I'm just asking.

DAVID: Yeah, they said it just lifts off.

HELEN: Hmm.

RACHEL: No. Way. We are not taking the lid off.

HELEN: Of course not.

Pause.

DAVID: I hope that coffee table holds up.

Pause.

HELEN: Sure it'll be fine.

Pause.

RACHEL: This is total and utter madness.

HELEN: Look, Rachel. I'm sorry if you don't approve. But I don't want him there, stuck in a freezer, all on his own. He always hated the cold. I'm aware that it's not terribly conventional or but it's what I want. I just want him here. With us.

DAVID: It's absolutely fine, Mum. Not a problem. Whatever you need. Right, Rach?

Rachel glares at him. Helen smiles and starts to open some of the sympathy cards on her lap.

RACHEL: (To David) Did you pay them?
DAVID: Yes.
RACHEL: How much?
DAVID: Don't worry about it.
RACHEL: Just tell me how much!
DAVID: (Quietly) Three thousand.
RACHEL: Three thousand pounds?? Show me the receipt?
DAVID: (Pulls an invoice from his pocket and reads) Ok, it was actually three thousand, four hundred and eighty-seven pounds. Plus VAT. But that does apparently include this very high-end casket in front of us, crematorium fees, a takeaway "Polytainer" urn, transport and some other stuff.
RACHEL: Transport?
DAVID: The hearse, I'm guessing. Unless you fancy sticking a roof rack on Mum's Nissan Micra.
RACHEL: What's the other stuff?
DAVID: (Cagey) Just other stuff.
RACHEL: Give me that. (Snatches the receipt off him and reads) "collection and care – nine hundred and seventy-five pounds"?! What? All they've done is pick him up and then … drop him off again.
DAVID: We had to pay a bit extra, didn't we?
RACHEL: Extra? For what? A solid gold urn? A tomb in Westminster Abbey?
DAVID: (Quietly) Embalming.
RACHEL: Sorry?
DAVID: (Louder, glancing at Helen, not wanting her to hear) Embalming. So that, you know, he's "preserved". While he's here.

Rachel stares at him in horror. David mistakes it for confusion.

DAVID: Apparently it's a relatively simple process. They just –
RACHEL: I know what it is, David!

Pause.

DAVID: Anyway, they were really nice guys. Said they'd be back next week to pick him up.

Helen stands up, puts the cards to one side and frowns at the coffin. She stands back from it and sizes it up for a moment, her brow furrowed. She shakes her head.

HELEN: Does this coffin look small to you?
RACHEL: It looks pretty standard, Mum.
HELEN: It looks a bit small to me.

RACHEL: I'm sure it's the right size.

HELEN: Do people shrink when they die?

RACHEL: Eventually, Mum.

DAVID: Nails and hair keep growing, don't they though? Like in Salem's Lot? When the vampire comes out of its coffin with its long nails and scratches on the window pane? (He shudders at the memory) Terrifying.

Rachel gives him a look that suggests he should be quiet immediately.

HELEN: (To Rachel) Did you remember to give them his glasses?

RACHEL: Yes. They're in his jacket pocket.

HELEN: Good, he was always losing them.

David stands up and takes a photo of the coffin on his phone. Rachel watches him, horrified.

RACHEL: What are you doing?

DAVID: Instagram.

RACHEL: David!

DAVID: Hashtag "dadshome!"

RACHEL: Stop it!

David sighs and puts his phone away. Rachel glares at him.

RACHEL: Idiot.

David takes a flat cap from his back pocket and puts it on. Helen nods approvingly at David and squeezes his arm affectionately. Rachel looks at him with narrowed eyes.

DAVID: Mum said I should take something of Dad's so it was this or the yellow trousers.

HELEN: It suits you, darling!

RACHEL: Wise choice. I'm not sure you'd want the yellow trousers now.

DAVID: Why not?

She gestures towards the coffin.

RACHEL: He's wearing them.

DAVID: Is he? Good on him. To the yellow trousers. They will be missed.

David raises his mug in a silent toast to the yellow trousers. Helen stands up, moves closer to the coffin. She runs her hand gently along the surface.

HELEN: So I've been thinking.

Pause.

HELEN: I want to see him.

David and Rachel stare at her.

DAVID: Now? In there?
HELEN: Yes.

David thinks about it for a second and then puts his mug down decisively.

DAVID: Ok then.
RACHEL: What? David, stay where you are! Mum, this is a really terrible idea.
DAVID: It's up to Mum, Rach.
HELEN: (Indecisive) No, maybe she's right. It is a terrible idea, isn't it? I
    shouldn't have even brought him back here. It's what mad people do.
DAVID: You're not mad. This isn't that mad. I think it's ok that he's back here in
    our living room because you didn't want him to be on his own. Or get cold.
    And it's ok to want to see his face again. Of course it is! You do what you
    want to do.
HELEN: Right then. I want to see him.
RACHEL: Mum, please! This is too much. It's morbid!
HELEN: It's not morbid. It's your father!

Pause.

HELEN: Besides, what if it's not him?

Rachel and David stare at her.

RACHEL: What?
HELEN: Someone needs to check!
DAVID: I'm pretty sure it's him, Mum.
HELEN: But what if it isn't? I read this story in the paper just last week. Two
    bodies got mixed up in the morgue. It happens all the time apparently. I
    think the family only found out they'd cremated the wrong woman because
    they found a metal leg at the other end. In the "ashes". (She shudders) And
    of course their poor dead mother didn't have a metal leg. Next thing, the
    police are involved and you're on page 6 of the Daily Mail. I'm just saying,
    these things happen. It could be anyone in there. And I'm sorry but this
    coffin looks a bit too short to me.
RACHEL: Mum, you're being absolutely mental.
HELEN: It's what your father would want.
RACHEL: It's not what he'd want. He'd want you to let him rest in peace.
DAVID: Rach, you don't have to look. It's just Dad.

Pause.

DAVID: Probably....

Rachel gives up and turns her back to both of them, covering her eyes with her hands. David starts to lift up the lid with some effort.

RACHEL: I cannot believe you're doing this. It's so degrading, you both gawping at him in his coffin.

DAVID: Ok! I've got it. You ready, Mum? You sure you want to do this?

HELEN: Yes. Do it. Before I change my mind. Open it.

He raises the lid of the coffin. They both stare inside. Moments pass. Rachel cannot bear it any longer.

RACHEL: Well? What?

She marches over and looks into the coffin herself. She's unable to tear her eyes away.

RACHEL: Oh. It doesn't look like Dad. Oh my God. That's not Dad. You were right, Mum. I don't think it's him. His mouth looks all funny.

HELEN: (Sitting down, gently pulling Rachel with her) That's your Dad, love.

DAVID: Hi, Dad. Good to see you. You look bloody good in those trousers.

RACHEL: Put the lid down.

DAVID: Did he get a haircut? His hair looks different.

RACHEL: Put the lid down.

DAVID: Don't you want to say anything?

RACHEL: Put the fucking lid down, David!!

David closes the lid of the coffin. They all sit in silence.

RACHEL: I took him to get his hair cut last week. To Giovanni's. When we were leaving, he gave Dad this massive hug. I didn't think anything of it. He's Italian – they're all a bit huggy, aren't they? But we got back to the car and I heard this noise. And it was Dad. He was crying. Not crying. Sobbing. And eventually he said that Giovanni had never hugged him before and it was because he knew he'd never see him again. I didn't know what to say. Because he was right, wasn't he? Dad knew it, I knew it, even bloody Giovanni knew it. I couldn't think of a single thing to make him feel better. So we just sat there. In the Tesco car park. And I can't stop thinking about it. I let him down.

Helen sits next to Rachel on the sofa. She puts her arm around her daughter.

HELEN: Rachel, you didn't let him down. You were there. He wasn't alone. That's all he needed and that's all that matters.

All three sit in silence for a while. Finally, David speaks.

DAVID: Last week, when they said Dad didn't have very long, I went into his room. He was pretty out of it with all the morphine but I got on the bed and I curled up next to him. I thought "this might be my last chance to say goodbye to him" so I really needed to not mess it up. So I just held his hand for a while, listened to the sound of him breathing and then I told him that I loved him.

RACHEL: Did he say anything?

DAVID: Yeah. He said, "I love you too, Helen."

Pause.

DAVID: And then he squeezed my arse.

Helen bursts out laughing.

RACHEL: He did not!

DAVID: He did! He was so out of it he thought I was bloody Mum! The worst thing was I didn't want to upset him by letting on it was actually me so I just lay there like a statue for what seemed like an eternity, hoping there'd be no more arse-squeezing!

RACHEL: Was there?

DAVID: No! He went to sleep, thank God. Want me to talk about this in the eulogy, Mum?

HELEN: (Smiling) Best not, darling.

Pause.

HELEN: He was a funny man, wasn't he? I can't quite believe he's gone. Thirty years. Goes by in a flash and all you're left with is the memory of them.

Rachel squeezes her mum's hand. David puts his arm around her.

RACHEL: I never thought I'd say this but I'm glad we get to keep him to ourselves for a bit longer. It's kind of nice we get to say goodbye like this.

Pause.

RACHEL: Nice but also super weird.

Pause.

RACHEL: And I'm sorry I called you mental.

HELEN: It's fine. I'm sure I am, a little bit. It's like being in a little bubble where the completely absurd seem entirely acceptable.

DAVID: We'll probably look back on this one day and say "did we really keep Dad's coffin in the living room for a week?"

They are all sitting back on the sofa again, this time happily squashed together. They sit quietly with their own thoughts for a moment.

HELEN: (Without moving) I should probably make a start on lunch really. Or I could just dig out one of those nice cottage pies that Julie made for us?

Unnoticed by Helen, Rachel and David's facial expressions briefly betray their true feelings towards Julie's cottage pies.

RACHEL: In a minute, Mum.

Rachel gently rests her head on Helen's shoulder. David covers Helen's hand with his own.

RACHEL: In a minute.

The three of them remain exactly where they are. "Here Comes The Sun" by The Beatles begins to play.

Slowly, the lights fade.

Ends.

Afterword

Vicki Connerty

When my father died at home after a relatively short but characteristically valiant battle with cancer, my mother insisted that the funeral director return him to us, coffin and all, the following day. Not for religious or traditional reasons but simply because she couldn't bear the idea of him being all on his own in a freezer. So, for the ten days prior to his funeral, we kept my Dad and his coffin in our little living room. As you do.

I never imagined that fifteen years later I would end up writing my very first short play about those surreal ten days. Nor did I imagine that my beloved Dad and his famed yellow trousers would eventually be immortalised in print. *Come Die With Me* is a little play about loss, love and, of course, laughter – the very best cure of all for broken hearts. It's about my family but it's for my Dad. I think he'd have liked it.

22 *Hurricane Blues*

Daisy Stenham

Characters
OLIVE, *mid-forties.*
MARGOT, *early forties.*
FRANNY, *mid-thirties.*
MABEL, *8 years old.*

Note
(–) at the end of a line indicates being cut off.
(…) indicates where speech trails off.
(Beat) indicates a brief break in the dialogue.
(Pause) indicates where there is a thought process happening.

Original production details
Hurricane Blues was commissioned and produced at Southwark Playhouse by
Little Pieces of Gold on 10 June 2018.

The cast was as follows:

OLIVE	Gemma Seren
MARGOT	Beth Eyre
FRANNY	Hannah Marsters
MABEL	Laura Pieters
Director:	Charlotte Vickers

*Olive sits at her mother's kitchen table smoking, staring into space. A piece of
paper, a pen, an ash-tray, a bottle of whisky and a half-drunk glass are in front
of her – the rest of the stage is empty. Off-stage, the front door slams and Margot
enters and looks around, confused.*

MARGOT: Where's the kitchen?
OLIVE: Oh good, you noticed. I packed it away – you can thank me later.
MARGOT: But we didn't go through it?
OLIVE: Right, well, there's a dead mouse, half a bottle of whisky, a Pret bag full
of Valium, some overflowing ashtrays and a bunch of M&S coffee filters –

Ecuadorian fair trade, strength four, I think. (Beat) That's about it. We can divvy up the treasure later when Franny gets here.

Margot ignores her, picks up the glass of whisky and takes a swig as Olive walks off-stage. Olive returns with a box and bubble wrap.

OLIVE: You know what? I've been thinking, if you actually gutted it, put a lick of paint on the walls, ripped up this floor, knocked down that wall, you could make a killing.
MARGOT: Jesus, Olive. She's barely cold.
OLIVE: I'm just thinking practically.

Olive lays the box down on the floor and gestures to it.

OLIVE: There.

Olive sits back at the table and takes a drag of her cigarette. Margot crouches down and opens the box, looking perplexed as she brings out endless overflowing ashtrays in varying shapes and sizes – the odd novelty one.

MARGOT: You could always rationalise yourself out of a crisis. Remember when we were kids and she got a restraining order for throwing a brick through the window and you said it was ok, because at least now you had something to write about? (Beat) What was the play called again?

Olive smiles.

OLIVE: "Love Hurts". (Beat) You played Mum brilliantly.

The mouse runs out. Margot screams.

OLIVE: Maybe the mouse isn't dead. Look if you want a job, you can bring in the box marked "living room" from the hall and see if you want to keep anything.

Margot exits, Olive kneels down and examines the floor. Seconds later Margot enters with the box, she sits back down on the floor pulling out books and DVDS. Olive sits back at the table and writes. Margot suddenly brings out a wig, which she reflexively chucks across the room.

MARGOT: Oh god it's her wig!

Olive doesn't look up.

OLIVE: Take it you don't want to keep that.

Beat.

MARGOT: Only she would pretend to have cancer, to get out of jury service.
OLIVE: It worked.

They crack a smile. Margot keeps sorting, Olive writing. After a moment Olive puts down the pen exasperated.

OLIVE: Margot, you have to do it. (Beat) Speak.
MARGOT: Why?
OLIVE: It's what she would have wanted.
MARGOT: Well I am sorry but she lost those privileges –
OLIVE: Margot, for God's sake you're forty-one – enough with the violins. She's your mother, we all have a responsibility to her, especially now. If you won't do the eulogy you could read a poem? That's minimal commitment surely. I've brought some print-outs for inspiration.
MARGOT: Of course you have –

Olive slams her rather large statement handbag on the table and brings out some printed-out poems – in different coloured plastic wallets.

OLIVE: Carol Ann Duffy –
MARGOT: Jesus.
OLIVE: Auden: "Funeral Blues". You know that one from Four Weddings and a Funeral. The one that goes "Stop all the clocks, cut off the telephone –"

Margot pauses, mid-sorting.

MARGOT: Olive, I can't read that, I didn't speak to her for five years. I literally "cut off the telephone" to her. How unbelievably inappropriate would that be?
OLIVE: Hector thinks –
MARGOT: Oh don't bring Mr Happy into it. (Beat) He's not coming today is he?
OLIVE: (Nonchalantly) He might swing by with a lasagne later, but no concrete promises were made.
MARGOT: When will people understand that in death, no one, ever, wants to eat a lasagne?
OLIVE: It's some cashew nut one. Mabel's vegan now. Can you believe it? She's eight.

Olive brings out a compact crowbar from her handbag and gets down on her knees.

MARGOT: What on earth are you doing?
OLIVE: I have always wanted to know what's under this floor.

Olive gets to work with the crowbar.

MARGOT: Why can't Franny do it?
OLIVE: What? I can't hear you!

Olive lifts up a floorboard. She sighs.

(To herself) Plywood, how disappointing.

Olive gets up and puts the crowbar on the table.

MARGOT: Franny?
OLIVE: What?
MARGOT: The eulogy, why can't she do it?

Olive, still standing, picks up her glass of whisky, takes a sip.

OLIVE: I think it would be too much for her right now. She's struggling –

Margot stops unpacking, sits at the table, gets out one of Olive's cigarettes.

MARGOT: Her mother's just died.
OLIVE: Our mother.
MARGOT: Yes. (Beat) God, it's the first time I've said it out loud. (Beat) Sounds
    ugly doesn't it?

Margot lights the cigarette, takes a drag. Olive, still standing, looks around.

OLIVE: I'll make a round of tea, the priest will be here soon.

Olive wanders away, holding the glass.

MARGOT: Considering none of us are remotely religious I have no idea why you
    invited a priest over.
OLIVE: To talk us through the service. It's comforting. (Beat) And actually she
    had a Catholic upbringing, so you never know.
MARGOT: Where did you find him?
OLIVE: (Pleased with herself) Her.
MARGOT: Where did you find "her"?
OLIVE: Where anyone finds anything: online. (Beat) I'll make a round of tea.

Margot swigs from the whisky bottle.

MARGOT: Good luck finding a mug that hasn't been ashed in.

Olive looks around.

OLIVE: Ah, there's no milk.

MARGOT: She didn't really believe in soft drinks. (Beat) Just drink the whisky, it does the trick.

Olive ignores her.

OLIVE: So I sort of thought, in the eulogy, we could add a few things, you know jazz it up a bit?

MARGOT: Like what?

OLIVE: (Gets her piece of paper from the table) I thought we could describe her as an "active member of her community".

Margot stares at her in disbelief, followed by a loud noise from above.

MARGOT: Oh my god! Did you hear that? (Margot gets up) I think someone's upstairs! (More noise) Oh my god, do you think it's an intruder? Olive, get the crowbar.

OLIVE: It's not an intruder.

MARGOT: (Whispers) How do you know? (Beat) Don't go there with any spirit talk.

OLIVE: Don't be angry.

Beat.

MARGOT: What?

Pause.

MARGOT: Olive?

OLIVE: It's an estate agent. (Beat) They're just doing a vague appraisal, taking some photos. This was the only morning they could do it.

MARGOT: Jesus, already? You're unbelievable. Have you told Franny?

Pause.

MARGOT: So you're lying to her?

OLIVE: No I am phasing in the truth – there's a difference. Look, she's in shock, but obviously she can't live here. The place would be on fire in a week. It's an insane idea. (Beat) She needs to move in with you.

MARGOT: What?

OLIVE: Yes.

MARGOT: No!

OLIVE: Yes. Just for a while, while she finds her feet. She can't be alone right now. And she certainly can't be here.

MARGOT: Why can't she stay with you!

OLIVE: (As if obvious) The kids can't be living with a recovering alcoholic.

Margot shoots her a look.

OLIVE: I am sorry I didn't mean to –

Margot is silent, a pause.

OLIVE: (Softly) You know, selling this place – the money, it would be freedom for all of us, it could really help. It would be good for Franny too, get her set up. (Beat) And you, if you're still thinking of –

MARGOT: I really don't want to talk about that right now. (Pause, sits back at the table) I feel guilty Olive, for cutting her off.

Olive sighs, continues sorting the box Margot left.

OLIVE: You did what you had to at the time. People get too sentimental in death. She was no saint.

MARGOT: I know, but that seems so irrelevant now. She was also so much more. (Beat) It's funny, I spent so long trying to calibrate how I felt about her, trying to work out why she did certain things, was it her fault or not, trying to work out where it all went wrong. Tracing events in linear time as if her story, as if she, could be understood so simply, so crudely – that I lost the grey in-between. (Beat) It's what we do though isn't it? We try to give things a form, a context – we try to understand people, grapple for a thread of reason in the dark. Because narrative, story, is what's meant to redeem us, heal us, anoint us. (Beat) And then I realised one day, why bother? It wasn't depressing so much as liberating. Because I realised I would never know, that try as I might, I would never understand her. And maybe that's ok. (Pause) I think if I really did, it would somehow hurt more.

OLIVE: Best not to dwell on it. Dwelling never got anyone anywhere. You know what we should be striving for? (Beat) To be like that mouse: blissfully, pathologically, in the present….

MARGOT: You don't have to worry, I think I'm "pathologically" aware of our present condition as it is.

Offstage the front door slams. Olive mouths "FUCK".

MARGOT: (Shouts out) Franny?

Franny enters, looks around confused.

OLIVE: You're early?

FRANNY: What have you done to the kitchen?

OLIVE: I just packed it up, I haven't thrown anything.

FRANNY: Well, I'm unpacking it. You can't just bulldoze in here and pack everything away, erase all memory....

Franny heads to the boxes, throwing out more books, DVDS, ornaments.

OLIVE: (Eyes Franny) Have you had a drink?

FRANNY: Sure, I had two cups of coffee, a flat can of Sprite, and a glass of water. The water was two-thirds Bourbon, if that's what you meant? (Beat) And what about you, taken a piss today?

Margot rolls her eyes. More noise from upstairs.

FRANNY: Is someone up there?

MARGOT: (Quickly) It's Olive's priest, she's –

OLIVE: Blessing the house.

FRANNY: Why?

MARGOT: (Swigs more whiskey) Apparently it's a service they offer now.

FRANNY: Well, she shouldn't be up there. No one should.

Franny is about to exit, Margot pulls her back.

MARGOT: I'll go. You're right. (Looks at Olive) NO ONE should be up there.

OLIVE: (Shouting after her) And bring her coffee mug down, we need them!

Margot exits. Olive returns to the table. Franny starts going through the "kitchen" box.

OLIVE: There's nothing important. You wouldn't want....

Franny picks out the Pret bag of Valium and shakes it.

OLIVE: Those are mine.

FRANNY: As if.

OLIVE: Franny, hand them over.

FRANNY: I will share them out three ways as is fair – with everything concerning this house.

OLIVE: Those are mine. Don't you dare take one!

FRANNY: Oh, really? And what are you going to do, come at me with your crowbar?

Olive shoots her a look.

FRANNY: And what are you doing with a bag of baby blues anyway? Mr Happy finally bringing you down?

OLIVE: Can everyone STOP calling him that. (Beat) He's not, he's depressed.

FRANNY: The life coach is depressed?

OLIVE: Don't, the irony is not lost on me.

FRANNY: Since when?

OLIVE: I'd rather not talk about it. Can you just help me find some more mugs?

FRANNY: (Gestures to the pills) Maybe you could do with one of these? Take the edge off –

OLIVE: Stop it. No one's taking anything. There's a priest upstairs.

FRANNY: (About to take a pill) Exactly.

Before Franny can take one, Olive grabs the bag out of her hands, chucks them on the floor and starts stamping on them aggressively, crushing them up. Franny stares in shock. Margot enters and looks at the bag. A pause.

MARGOT: Lucky mouse.

OLIVE: (Brightly, to Margot) All ok up there?

MARGOT: Yes, she even said she might come back tomorrow, to finish up.

OLIVE: That sounds positive.

FRANNY: How long does it take to bless a house?

MARGOT: She's very busy this time of year. Apparently there's a real market for it.

FRANNY: God, everyone's lost their minds!

MARGOT: She's going to let herself out. It felt so strange standing in her bedroom, like that feeling when you're little and you go on holiday and then you come back and your room seems oddly still, like a set, lifeless, and it's all so underwhelming. (Beat) I don't know what I expected.

Margot sits back at the table and lights another cigarette.

OLIVE: Right, well, now we are all together, another thing I want to go through. Mabel wants to do a performance, at the service –

FRANNY: You can say funeral.

OLIVE: It's a dance to a song that apparently reminds her of Mum. I don't know where she has got the idea from, but Hector is adamant she is allowed a platform to express her grief –

MARGOT: What's the song?

OLIVE: Bear with me.

Olive gets out her phone and plays the opening bars of "Dancing Queen" by ABBA. After it ends, a moment of stunned silence.

OLIVE: I mean I know it's not ideal, but she's been practicing for days, and to be honest I'm sick of controlling people.

Franny snorts.

OLIVE: (Breezily) Besides, it's unconventional, maybe she would like it.
FRANNY: Well if we're allowing that, I can't see why I can't read my eulogy.

Franny gets up on the kitchen table.

OLIVE: Not if you've been drinking –
FRANNY: When you were at your best, you were the best in the room. A life force, a –
MARGOT: (Looking up at her) If you're willing to read a shit Carol Anne Duffy
poem she'll let you speak.
OLIVE: Margot!

Franny ignores them. Off-stage the front door slams.

FRANNY: Sort of rude to do a bless and run no? (Beat) Well, I guess now I can
really speak freely. But at your worst –
MARGOT: Christ.
OLIVE: No, Franny we're keeping it light! (Grabs her legs) Get off the table, it's –
FRANNY: But it isn't light! Far from light. She's dead and we are meant to "keep
it light". God forbid anyone is actually allowed to feel anything in your
presence. (Beat) Face so pinched it's like you're drowning in vinegar.
MARGOT: Franny you're drunk.
OLIVE: (To Franny) Oh just say what you clearly want to say.

Franny gets down.

FRANNY: I can't believe you can think about selling this place now. Mabel let it
slip yesterday in the car. You should have seen Hector's face, looked like he
had seen a ghost. That, or he was severely constipated.
MARGOT: Oh grow up Franny! She's thinking of you. We're always fucking
thinking of you.
How are you going to live? You need money, resources, you basically need a
full-time nanny. (Beat) That was an estate agent upstairs, taking photos, not
a priest. Yes, Olive wants to sell and to be honest I would quite like to be
shot of this place – it's hardly a sanctuary of fond memories.
OLIVE: It's only practical.
FRANNY: (To Olive) Why did you lie to me?
OLIVE: I don't know, soften the blow I guess.

A pause. Franny turns away.

FRANNY: I didn't see her for three months.

Beat.

OLIVE: I did what I thought was best –

FRANNY: No you meddled and you controlled – what you always do. And what you're doing right fucking now, selling this house, packing it all away, packing her away.

Franny starts throwing more things out of the boxes.

MARGOT: She got you into treatment Franny –

FRANNY: Forced me into it.

OLIVE: Oh I am sorry, you're right. I should have waited patiently until you were ready to skip up in there yourself!

FRANNY: You should have left me alone.

Beat.

FRANNY: I was ok, I could manage.

MARGOT: You were a mess.

OLIVE: You needed help Franny. (Beat) I, we, were trying to protect you.

FRANNY: No one asked you to.

OLIVE: That's not how it works. (Sighs) I didn't know this was going to happen Franny. None of us did. It was an accident. (Beat) A really unfortunate accident –

FRANNY: I should have been here –

OLIVE: It wouldn't have made a difference. (Beat) There's no point festering over it.

FRANNY: (Quietly) I don't want anyone to know she was drunk when she fell.

OLIVE: Well I certainly wasn't planning on broadcasting it. Now, come on, let's get on and sort the rest of this charity pile before Hector gets here – we're behind as it is. (Goes to the DVDs) Do either of you want to keep any of these DVDS? Say now, or they're going in the pile? Franny? Margot?

Franny stares at her in disbelief. Margot shakes her head apprehensively. Olive picks up a DVD from the pile.

OLIVE: Any of these? (Beat) Want it? None of them are scratched, I double checked, so they're perfectly good to re-watch. Franny?

Franny continues staring.

OLIVE: (To Franny) What?

FRANNY: I just want you to show some semblance of a feeling, some scrap of evidence that you care, that she mattered. Something, anything. "No, let's just be brave, let's just keep it together, organise, make calls, pack everything away, send round-robin emails about the summer cottage and storage quotes. Should we have one or two vegetarian options at the wake? Clear spirits or dark? Who's chipping in for the memorial sundial?" Christ, you're acting like you're organising a fucking wedding. And nobody cares! Nobody cares about any of this shit – least of all the fucking DVDS. God, doesn't it get exhausting, being so relentlessly pragmatic? Don't you ever get sick of it, pretending to give a shit about this stuff all the time?

OLIVE: Because what other option is there? Just stop? Give up? Walk off-stage? Give in to the hurricane I am feeling inside? I am trying to stay in the room, in the world, it's not brave, it's surviving. It's saying "I am still playing the game" or trying to – and you have to work from the bottom up, the little things, the minutiae. Because all those infinite little tasks – on their own mundane seeming, irrelevant, superficial – all add up to form a bigger picture, that you're still in, invested, that you have some kind of hope for what's ahead. (Beat) Because we know how fragile it all is. We know what it looks like when the order is subverted, cracked, turned upside down, inside out. We know how quickly someone can spiral. (Beat) And most people don't notice the importance of all these infinite little tasks, the value of normality, until it's gone, collapsed in at the seams, the coordinates of the day scrambled. Then people notice. Then people get upset. When it's four o'clock in the afternoon and someone hasn't got dressed. When the bedsheets are dirty, the ashtrays spilling over, the peaches in the fruit bowl have started to rot from the inside out. Suddenly "ordinary" takes on a new currency. (Beat) So I am just trying to stay in the room, in the world, but that doesn't mean that I don't care that I somehow "got away with it". Because we all have an inner life, and sometimes it's so far from what you see on the outside – we will forever be somewhat, slightly, lost in translation. (Beat) So I am not trying to forget to ignore. I'm just trying to stay hopeful. (Beat) I am just trying to stay in the game. But don't for a second think that it's easy.

A pause. Off-stage the doorbell rings.

OLIVE: If it's the real priest tell her to fuck off.

Margot exits to answer the door.

OLIVE: What was I meant to do? It broke my heart that I failed you. I thought you were going to be ok. I know you were angry and you found things difficult. I know it wasn't easy growing up here, around her, but I thought we did enough, that I did enough. (Beat) I thought you were going to be ok.

FRANNY: (Quietly) I know, I am sorry. (Beat) But I'm trying.

Olive's eyes water. Margot returns with Mabel who looks around scared.

OLIVE: (Shocked) Mabel?

MABEL: Mummy are you ok? What's going on?

FRANNY: (Goes up to her, tenderly) It's ok darling. It all got messy in here because we were practising your fantastic dance for Grandma.

Olive and Margot exchange a look.

MABEL: Really? You're going to do it with me?

FRANNY: Why not? We're super impressed.

MABEL: You know the moves?

FRANNY: Well, Mum's in the middle of teaching us, but you know she has two left feet, so will you show us how to do it? Put it on Margot would you?

Margot puts back on "Dancing Queen". Mabel starts doing the dance routine, Olive gets up and stands next to her and joins in, so do Margot and Franny. They all stand in a line, copying Olive and Mabel's steps.

Afterword

Daisy Stenham

In writing *Hurricane Blues* I was interested in exploring the nebulous space following the immediate aftermath of a family death. I wanted to investigate the subjective and nuanced experience of grief; how three sisters can have an entirely different understanding of their mother. Mental health is a big theme in the play and I set out to examine the complexity of children navigating a complicated parental love. Inspired by plays such as *August: Osage County*, I wanted to write about the coming together of siblings under difficult circumstances.